The Olympic Games:
The First Thousand Years

Also by M. I. Finley

STUDIES IN LAND AND CREDIT IN ANCIENT ATHENS
THE WORLD OF ODYSSEUS
THE ANCIENT GREEKS
ASPECTS OF ANTIQUITY
ANCIENT SICILY: TO THE ARAB CONQUEST
EARLY GREECE: THE BRONZE AND ARCHAIC AGES
THE ANCIENT ECONOMY
DEMOCRACY ANCIENT AND MODERN
THE USE AND ABUSE OF HISTORY

Editor

THE GREEK HISTORIANS
SLAVERY IN CLASSICAL ANTIQUITY
ANCIENT CULTURE AND SOCIETY SERIES

Also by H. W. Pleket

EPIGRAPHICA

I. Texts on the Economic History of the Greek World
II. Texts on the Social History of the Greek World

THE GREEK INSCRIPTIONS IN THE RIJKSMUSEUM
VAN OUDHEDEN AT LEIDEN

THE OLYMPIC GAMES: THE FIRST THOUSAND YEARS

M. I. FINLEY
Professor of Ancient History
in the University of Cambridge

H. W. PLEKET
Reader in Greek and Latin Epigraphy
in the University of Leiden

1976
CHATTO & WINDUS
LONDON

Published by
Chatto & Windus Ltd
40 William IV Street
London WC2N 4DF

*

Clarke, Irwin & Co. Ltd
Toronto

ISBN 0 7011 2087 8

© M. I. Finley and H. W. Pleket 1976

Printed in Great Britain by
R. & R. Clark Ltd, Edinburgh

Preface

The first modern Olympic Games, in Athens in 1896, were inspired, as the name indicates, by the ancient Games held every four years in a rather pastoral, wholly non-urban setting at Olympia in western Greece. In this book, we have tried to give a rounded picture of the ancient Games in the course of their thousand-year history — the site, the contests, the athletes and spectators, the politics and the ideals. Although we have abstained from drawing many comparisons, and certainly from pointing to 'lessons', the interests of the modern reader and the experience of the modern Olympics have always been in view. We have therefore not merely described and reported (in text and illustrations); we have also asked the questions that are bound to come to mind to a reader in the second half of the twentieth century, and we have tried to suggest answers when possible.

The original evidence about the Olympic Games, as about Games in general in the ancient world, is fragmentary and widely scattered. Some of it is literary, some archaeological and epigraphical. No one can claim to have examined every scrap, but we have personally studied a large proportion and we have tried not to overlook any important ancient document or modern discussion. We take full scholarly responsibility for what we have written, although we have only exceptionally indicated a source.

In the absence of bibliographical indications, we should like to record our indebtedness to colleagues whose publications we have found indispensable: on Olympia itself, H.-V. Herrmann and A. Mallwitz; on the Games and the athletes, Joachim Ebert, the late H. A. Harris, Reinhold Merkelbach, Luigi Moretti, Louis Robert, and the three great pioneers, E. N. Gardiner and Julius Jüthner early in the present century, J. H. Krause in the nineteenth.

We should also like to thank Judy Lester for her assistance in procuring the illustrations and for the Index.

M. I. F.
H. W. P.

Contents

[vii]

Plates

PLATES

PLATES

COLOUR PLATES

[x]

MAPS

FIGURES

ACKNOWLEDGEMENTS

The authors and publishers wish to thank the following for permission to reproduce:

Antikenmuseum und Skulpturhalle, Basel: 2 (a).

Badisches Landesmuseum: 16 (a).

British Library Board: 26.

British Museum: 10 (a), 11 (a), 11 (b), 16 (b), 17 (a), 17 (b), 20, 21, 22 (b), 24 (c), 29 (a), 29 (b), 30 (a), 30 (b), IV and jacket, V (b), VII (b).

Professor O. Broneer: 18 (c).

Professor J. Délorme and Éditions E. de Boccard (*Gymnasion*): 28 (a).

Deutsches Archaeologisches Institut, Athens: 6 (b), 6 (d), 7 (a), 7 (b), 7 (c), 9 (b), 10 (c), 15 (b), 18 (a), 24 (b), 27.

Deutsches Archaeologisches Institut, Athens, and Prestel Verlag (A. Mallwitz, *Olympia und seine Bauten*): 4-5.

Deutsches Archaeologisches Institut, Rome: 3 (b).

École Française d'Archéologie, Athens: 25.

Fitzwilliam Museum: 6 (a), 10 (b), 23 (b), 23 (c), 23 (d), 30 (c).

Fogg Art Museum, Harvard University: Bequest of David M. Robinson (detail): 1 (b).

Fotomarburg: 6 (c), 19 (a).

Gabinetto Fotografico Nazionale, Rome: 31 (a).

Mrs. P. B. Gardiner and the Clarendon Press (E. N. Gardiner: *Athletics of the Ancient World*): Figs. 5, 6, 13, 16.

Greek Embassy Press and Information Office, London: 1 (a).

Mrs. H. A. Harris: 18 (b).

Professor H.-V. Herrmann and Carl Winter, Universitätsverlag: Figs. 7-10.

Hirmer Fotoarchiv: 8 (a), 8 (b), 9 (a), 13, 14, 19 (b), 23 (a), 32, I, II (b), III (a).

Mansell Collection: II (a), VIII.

Martin Wagner Museum, Würzburg: 31 (b).

Metropolitan Museum of Art, New York, Rogers Fund 1907: 12; Rogers Fund 1906: 22 (a); Rogers Fund 1914: VII (a) (14.130.12 Greek Vases).

Caecilia H. Moessner: III (b).

Musées Nationaux, Paris: 30 (d).

Museum of Fine Arts, Boston: 15 (a).

Rijksmuseum van Oudheden te Leiden: V (a) (PC8).

Staatliche Museen zu Berlin, DDR: VI and jacket.

Thames and Hudson Ltd. (Berve-Gruben-Hirmer: *Greek Temples, Theatres and Shrines*): 28 (b).

Verlag der Österreichischen Akademie, Vienna (J. Jüthner: *Die athletische Leibesübungen der Griechen*, 1968): Figs. 2, 3 (a) and (b).

Penguin Books Ltd.: *The Odes of Pindar* translated by C. M. Bowra (Penguin Classics 1969).

Note: Arabic numerals refer to the monochrome plates, and roman numerals refer to the colour plates.

A NOTE ON GREEK MEASURES
OF DISTANCE AND MONEY VALUES

The ancient Greek measures of length were based primarily on parts of the body, with the foot as the main unit. Unfortunately, neither the foot nor its subdivisions and multiples were stable, varying both in place and in time. The *stadion* (Latin *stadium*) was always 600 feet, and therefore varied according to the foot being used. At an early date the *stadion* became the standard distance for the sprint in racing, and soon the Stadium was also the race-track (but only in modern times an arena or sports-ground). Archaeological excavation has revealed that the Olympic *stadion* was 192·27 metres in length, the one for the Pythian Games at Delphi 177·5; others ranged from 181·3 to 210 metres. For convenience, we have used round numbers in our text: 200 metres for the Olympic sprint and multiples of 200 for the longer races.

The monetary systems, based on weights, were equally varied. The main unit of weight, the *mina*, was too large to be coined (as was the *talent*, 60 minas, in which tribute was often expressed, for example). For coining, the basic unit was $\frac{1}{100}$ of a mina, called a *drachma*; the coins most frequently minted were the drachma, the 2-drachma piece (called didrachm or stater), the four-drachma piece (tetradrachm) and the *obol* ($\frac{1}{6}$ of a drachma). The obol was usually coined in bronze, the others in silver. To appreciate the significance of the sums mentioned in this book, given the variations in local systems and in the purchasing power of money, we offer two comparative figures as guidelines: at the end of the fifth century B.C., each Athenian hoplite (heavy-armed infantryman) received a drachma a day while on duty, another for his batman, a sum which was then the average day's pay for a skilled workman, on which (say 275–300 drachmas a year) the latter could maintain a small family; under the Roman Empire, when the drachma was conventionally equated to the Roman *denarius*, a soldier's annual pay ranged from 225 to 300 drachmas.

TABLE OF DATES

[xiv]

TABLE OF DATES

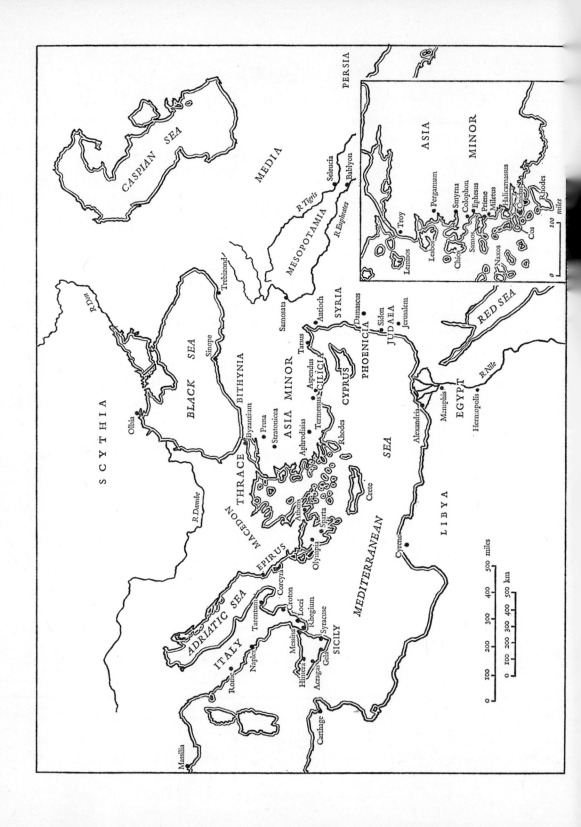

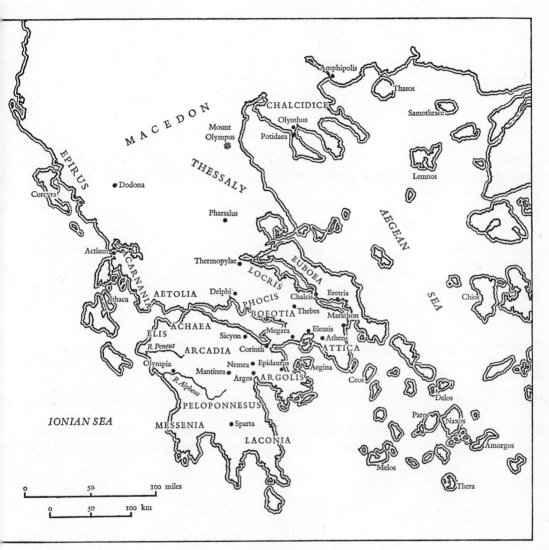

Map 2: The Greek Mainland.

1

Ancient and Modern

On September 1, 1870, France was heavily defeated at the battle of
Sedan, not eight weeks after Napoleon III had declared war on
Prussia. Three days later France was proclaimed a Republic; in
another ten days the city of Paris capitulated. This pair of disasters,
to which the subsequent loss of Alsace and Lorraine must be added,
brought deep, long-lasting gloom to the French. It also provided the
seed-bed in which the modern Olympic Games germinated.

The battle of Waterloo, it had been said and often repeated, was
won over Napoleon I on the playing-fields of Eton. The tragedy was
that the French *lycées* had an excessively intellectual programme; they
had no playing-fields, their pupils played no games and received little
physical training. That contrast became almost an obsession with
Pierre, baron de Coubertin, who was only eight years old when Sedan
was lost, and he had hardly come of age before he embarked on a
campaign to remedy the critical French weakness.

Born in a very wealthy, very Catholic, very ancient aristocratic
family, Coubertin believed in a natural élite. So he concentrated his
efforts on his country's 'gilded youth' (*jeunesse dorée*), as they were
popularly known. His models were the 'gilded youth' of two other
societies: the *ephebes* of ancient Greek cities, who spent much of their

time in the public gymnasia, where athletic and paramilitary activities and contests were punctuated, for those who wished them, with lectures by philosophers and itinerant orators; and, even more compelling, the public schools of contemporary England. *Tom Brown's School Days*, Taine's *Notes on England* and a visit, at the age of twenty, to Eton and Rugby, captivated him. Physical exercise and games, he argued again and again in speeches and in articles published by an association for physical education, were essential to a proper educational system. Through physical fitness, sound competition, true amateurism and the spirit of fair play, the natural élite of France, drawn from the aristocracy and the prosperous middle class, would provide their fatherland with new and inspired leadership at home and in the colonies overseas, would help recover the national self-consciousness and prestige shattered in the 1870 war.

For an élite, amateurism and fair play were, or should have been, obvious virtues and sufficient rewards in themselves; Coubertin spoke of 'the noble and chivalrous character of athletics', even of a 'religion of sport'. But how were the young to be won over? On his own testimony, Coubertin had been enthralled by the ancient Olympic Games in his boyhood, and he began to see practical possibilities in his youthful dreams. Why not re-create the Games? They would provide not only the right kind of model but also a valuable inducement. The prospect of Olympic championships, of winning medals—the modern equivalents of the ancient olive wreaths—would fire the imagination of the young and help convert them to the new vision.

Ironically, it was again the Germans who gave Coubertin the stimulus. The site of the ancient Olympic Games, which had completely disappeared in the Middle Ages, was discovered in 1766 by an English antiquary, Richard Chandler, while on a mission in Greece on behalf of the Society of Dilettanti. In 1829 a French team excavated the site for six weeks, but it was the Germans who made the real break-through. That story began in 1852, with a public lecture about Olympia, romantic, not very accurate, by Professor Ernst Curtius of the University of Berlin. In the audience were the Prussian ruler, Friedrich Wilhelm IV, and his son, the future Kaiser Wilhelm I, to whom Curtius had been tutor for a time. Twenty years later, after Wilhelm came to the throne of the new, unified Germany, negotiations with Greece produced a formal agreement whereby the German government undertook to bear the full cost of a large-scale excavation.

Between 1875 and 1881, under Curtius' direction, much of the monumental splendour of the ancient site was uncovered, though in ruins. Publication of the results of each year's excavation followed promptly, so that Coubertin, like others who had an interest in Olympia, could follow the discoveries in detail. And Coubertin, inspired by his dominant passion, quickly translated archaeology into an imaginative proposal. 'Germany', he wrote, 'has brought to light the remains of Olympia; why should France not succeed in reviving its ancient glory?'

Though an élitist, Coubertin was not a wholly typical French aristocrat of his time. He accepted the paternalistic views of contemporary 'social Catholicism' and foresaw a day when young men from the lower classes might share his new ideology of physical exercise and games. If compensation for lost earnings were necessary in order to involve them in Olympic competition, he would not oppose that. 'Inequality is more than a law,' he once wrote, 'it is a fact; and patronage is more than a virtue, it is a duty.'

Coubertin was also not a chauvinist. Though a French patriot, he divorced himself from the prevailing militaristic nationalism and he argued that a revived Olympic festival would further the cause of international understanding, brotherhood and peace. This did not make his task any easier: revenge, not amity, was the dominant slogan in leading French circles. There was powerful resistance to *international* games in which Germany, in particular, would participate. In the French sporting world there was also opposition to 'foreign influences': as late as 1901 one well known sportsman complained publicly, 'Having copied the Germans, we now copy the English. From one day to another, we unlearn our Frenchness.' And there was distaste, in the educational world as among aristocrats and gentlemen generally, for vulgar emphasis on sporting activities.

Nevertheless, by 1894 Coubertin had made sufficient progress to summon an international conference in Paris, at the Sorbonne, 'to study and propagate the principles of amateurism'. He then set off for Greece, and in October of that year he visited Olympia for the first time in his life. Two years later, in 1896, the first modern Olympic Games were held in Athens. Practical considerations of access and facilities for both athletes and spectators ruled Olympia out. Athens provided a new stadium with a seating capacity of nearly 50,000 (Plate 1a) as well as the desirable Greek background. Not much about these first modern Games, it should immediately be added, was genuinely 'Olympic'. There were forty-two events in ten sports with 285 participants, all men, and without team competitions except in gymnastics.* But only the running events, the long jump, the discus throw and wrestling were 'borrowed' from the original Games; the rest were either unknown to the ancients or were not included by them in their major Games. For all his romanticism, Coubertin had a contemporary aim, and the success of his scheme depended on a realistic choice of events—hurdling, cycling, the high jump, fencing and so on—appropriate to the athletic interests of his own day, not to those of a long dead civilization. It was the Olympic 'spirit', the Olympic ideology, as he conceived it, that was to serve his purposes, not the ancient Olympic reality.

There was nothing in ancient Greek practice, for example, to warrant the Olympic torch, carried halfway round the world as a symbol of Olympic internationalism. The torch races of antiquity were purely local relay races, with teams of naked men, wearing diadems, carrying their lighted torches in metal holders through the streets 'from altar to altar' (Plate 1b). They were part of a religious ritual in the strict sense, hence the diadems, the altars as end-points, and the climactic honour given the winner of placing his torch on the

* At Munich in 1972, there were 7147 competitors in twenty-one different sports (besides the winter sports, first introduced in 1924).

altar of the god or goddess being celebrated. Occasionally they were given a place in a Games festival, but never within the athletic programme proper. Nor did the ancients compete in races over very long distances. The marathon race has its origin in a famous legend: an Athenian, whose name is given differently in different versions of the tale—Phidippides in the most familiar account—ran the 42 kilometres to Marathon in order to join the battle against the invading Persians in 490 B.C., then ran back to Athens to bring news of the victory and dropped dead from his exertions.

It was fitting that the marathon race was won by a Greek in the first modern Games, to the delirious joy of the packed audience in the stadium (Plate 1a). Altogether, the United States and eight of the twelve participating European countries provided winners that year. Four came from France, five from Germany (as well as the co-winner in the tennis doubles). Coubertin's efforts had come to fruition, and he remained president of the International Olympic Committee until the completion of the 1924 Games. Only France refused to join in the acclaim. The French sporting press virtually ignored the Games, not only in 1896 but also in several succeeding meetings. The four French victories in 1896 were in traditional French sports, cycling and fencing, not in 'foreign importations'. When Coubertin died in 1937, he was financially bankrupt and, in the words of a biographer, 'one of the few Frenchmen left undecorated'.

The modern Olympics, as everyone knows, have produced not only heroes and spellbinding performances but also controversy, about amateurism, about over-emphasis, about politics. These the modern reader will have in the back of his mind when we turn to the past, to the world which first held Olympic Games. What were the events and the rules of the ancient Games, and how did they change? Who participated? How were they trained and rewarded? How were the Games managed? Were they then also the peak of an international network of sporting competitions, the goal of every dedicated amateur athlete? Were amateurism and professionalism an issue? What was the psychology, what were the values, among competitors, spectators and patrons? Was there criticism, and from what angles? Were the Games involved in politics, directly or indirectly, whether in local politics or in a wider arena?

As we tell the story, we shall resist the temptation to draw modern parallels or contrasts. Every reader will want to do that for himself. However, three distinctions had best be indicated at the beginning. First, the ancient Olympic programme became a restricted and stable one after a slow initial period of growth, as we shall see in detail in Chapter 3; all sorts of activities grew up on the fringe, but they were never incorporated into the official programme, the one that mattered. Second, whereas the modern Games change their venue every four years, the ancients never abandoned Olympia. Finally, and most re-markable, the ancient Olympics were held in every fourth summer without a break, despite wars and grave political difficulties at various times, until at least A.D. 261—more than 1000 years from their foundation, traditionally and credibly dated in 776 B.C. The modern Games, in contrast, have in their short existence been cancelled three times, in 1916, 1940 and 1944, because of two world wars.

The Greek world itself did not remain static for more than a thousand years. When the Olympic Games were established in 776 B.C., the Greeks were concentrated in a small area comprising the southern end of the Balkans, the islands of the Aegean Sea, and the coastal strip of Asia Minor (modern Turkey). In the same period, there began more than two centuries of steady migration, in small groups, westward to Sicily and southern Italy, along the Mediter-ranean coast to Marseilles in France and to Cyrene (Libya) in northern Africa; northeast along the coasts of the Black Sea; again later, after Alexander the Great (336-323 B.C.), to Egypt, Syria and Babylonia. In all this considerable area, the immigrants founded separate Greek communities and thought of themselves as proper Greeks in every sense ('Hellenes' in their own language, then as now: 'Greek' comes to us from the Latin name for them, 'Graeci'), not as Sicilians or Egyptians or Syrians. They all spoke Greek, with significant varia-tions only in dialect, worshipped the same gods in the same ways, organized their cultural life along the same lines, participated in the Olympic Games on an equal footing. But their common culture and their strong Hellenic consciousness never led them to unite into a single political system. 'Hellas' was thus not a country or a state but an abstraction, like Christendom in the Middle Ages or Islam today. The games were pan-Hellenic ('all-Greek') rather than, strictly speaking, international.

The Hellas of 776 B.C. was also very different institutionally from the Hellas of A.D. 261, quite apart from the geography. The Games were not immune from the changes that occurred, so that their history is an intricate mixture of tradition and permanence with subtle responses to what was going on outside. In 776 the small, autonomous, still largely illiterate communities in the original homeland were rather loosely organized under the dominance of aristocratic land-holding families, with poor natural resources and a low level of technology, yet already so overpopulated relatively, in some regions, as to stimulate the first western migrations in search of new lands to farm.

The next two or three centuries saw substantial progress and increasing differentiation in the economy and in social and political institutions. Many communities developed genuine urban centres—for example, Miletus, Athens, Corinth, Syracuse—with a rising volume of handicraft production and maritime trade, a higher standard of living, more and richer luxury products, able to support a denser population and to expend energy and means on literature and the fine arts. Improved and more frequent communication among the farflung sections of Hellas brought goods and ideas from one to the other, and helped to maintain the unity of language, culture and way of life we have already noted. Even those regions, including Elis, the district in which Olympia is situated, that remained predominantly agrarian and something of a backwater, were involved in these interchanges.

The more complex social structure, more wealth and improved technology helped bring about major changes in military and naval organization. In particular, from about 650 B.C. on, the massed phalanx of heavily armed infantrymen (known as 'hoplites' from the

Greek word for arms, *hopla*) became the dominant force in the army. Hoplite service was compulsory for every able-bodied citizen rich enough to equip himself with the requisite bronze armour—helmet, breastplate and greaves—and with shield, sword and spears (Plate IIIa). Archers, slingers and other more mobile, light-armed soldiers were used as auxiliaries, drawn almost exclusively from non-Greek peoples, such as Thracians and Scythians, employed by one or another Greek community as mercenaries. The cavalry, the aristocratic service *par excellence*, was reduced to the minor role of harassment of the phalanx and pursuit of hoplites in flight, except in such flat areas as the plain of Thessaly or parts of Sicily. Much of the Greek terrain, uneven, rocky, mountainous, was unsuitable for cavalry, and, besides, horses were difficult to feed and water during the long dry summer months in which nearly all warfare was conducted.

Clearly the old monopoly of political power in the hands of a small number of noble landowning families was bound to be challenged under the new economic, social and military conditions. Everywhere there was an advance in political organization. The more backward regions, such as Thessaly or Aetolia, tended to retain looser tribal federations, with a simpler social structure of aristocrats and non-aristocrats. But in the more advanced urban communities, continuous and often bitter struggles for political rights and political power set in as early as the seventh century B.C.

At one end of the political spectrum stood the autocratic rule of a single man or family, which the Greeks called 'tyranny'—the Cypselids in Corinth, Pisistratus, followed by his sons after his death, in Athens, Polycrates in Samos, all in the sixth century; the tyrants of Acragas and Syracuse who dominated the history of Greek Sicily from the mid-sixth century, apart from an interlude in the fifth, until the Romans conquered the island in the third; numerous others in Asia Minor, the Aegean islands and Cyrene. On the mainland of Greece, tyranny was not long-lasting and was overthrown, to be followed either by an oligarchical system, as in Corinth, or by a democracy. Each of these types, oligarchy and democracy, showed many variations, and not rarely succeeded each other within the same community time and again, following a civil war. The most stable democracy was the Athenian, first established in 508 B.C. and then developing, in the course of the next half-century, into a complex system of direct participation in the government by every citizen who so wished, at one level or another.

Whatever the form of government, each community—the Greek word was *polis*, conventionally translated as 'city-state'—was in principle an autonomous state, consisting of the city proper and its rural hinterland. In reality, the more powerful communities did not resist the temptation to dominate others, and sometimes to subjugate them. Sparta, for example, had seized the district of Messenia as early as the eighth century B.C., and in the course of the sixth century brought most of the rest of the Peloponnese, with the notable exception of Argos, into a league which she led. In the fifth century, Athens created a tribute-paying maritime empire that included, at its height, most of the Aegean islands, the coastal cities of Asia Minor and some others. And in Elis itself, as we shall see, similar moves, though on a much smaller scale, decided who would control the Olympic Games.

Whatever the form of government, too, communities were not egalitarian. Apart from the slaves, whose numbers began to swell substantially from the sixth century on, there were clear lines of demarcation among the citizens themselves, between rich and poor, between townsmen and peasants, between members of old, self-consciously aristocratic families and the *nouveaux riches*. Even in Athens, the most fully democratic state of the ancient world, there were men, such as the young, flashy, very rich, militarily able and politically ambitious Alcibiades (of whom we shall learn in some detail in Chapter 8), who thought of themselves and comported themselves as privileged aristocrats, and who were so recognized by their compatriots.

For the first 450 years, in sum, the Olympic Games were part of a city-state world. The next stage was initiated late in the fourth century B.C. from a rather surprising region, mountainous Macedon in the northeastern corner of the Greek peninsula. Although they were racially and linguistically kin to the Greeks, the Macedonians were considered to be outside Hellas, not part of it. However, their kings and aristocrats had become culturally Hellenized by the fifth century B.C., and they involved themselves more and more in Greek affairs until a League of the Hellenes was created in 338 B.C. under the leadership of the then Macedonian king, Philip II. He was assassinated in 336 B.C., whereupon his twenty-year-old son, Alexander, immediately embarked on a spectacular reign of thirteen years, during which he conquered the Persian Empire and parts of India.

There followed a migration of Greeks and Macedonians into the ancient centres of Near Eastern civilization, notably Egypt and Syria. New territorial states were established in the Near East, as well as in Asia Minor, under autocratic monarchs, nearly all of them Alexander's more successful generals and their descendants. The Greeks and Macedonians together formed a closed ruling class in the conquered lands, founded Greek cities (Alexandria and Antioch, for example) and continued their Greek culture, while the subject natives retained their own languages and ways of life, though gradually the élite among them became Hellenized and were accepted into Hellas, and therefore into the Olympic Games, too.

The final stage was again one of conquest, this time by the Romans, over a period of some two centuries beginning with the seizure of Sicily late in the third century B.C., followed by the conversion of the old Greek mainland into a Roman province in 146 B.C., and ultimately the conversion of the Roman state from a republic to an autocratic monarchy under Caesar's adopted son, Augustus, after he defeated Antony and Cleopatra at the battle of Actium in 31 B.C. Roman expansion did not end even then, but its subsequent history is not relevant to the Olympic story. At one moment, at the death of the emperor Trajan in A.D. 117, the empire covered an area of some 4,500,000 sq km, approximately half the land mass of the United States today, with a population of 50-60,000,000, roughly that of the

PLATE I Olympia today. The view is from a hill to the west.
The palaestra, with its columns, can be seen in the centre, and the
Hill of Cronus is at the top left (see also Figs. 7-10).

PLATE II (a) Bronze statue of a charioteer, 1·8 m high, found in Delphi in three pieces in 1896. The original monument, which stood near the temple of Apollo, included the chariot drawn by four horses, but only small fragments of these have survived. Parts of the inscribed base have also been recovered, revealing that the monument was dedicated to Apollo to commemorate victory in the Pythian Games by Polyzalus, tyrant of Gela in Sicily, probably in 474 B.C. Comparable statues were erected in Olympia, but archaeological excavation has so far failed to recover one.

(b) The two-horse chariot race in the Games staged by Achilles at the funeral of his friend Patroclus, described graphically in Homer's *Iliad* (see pp. 29–30). The inscription in the centre reads: 'Sophilus painted me. Patroclus' Games', and at the extreme right behind the spectators' stand the name 'Achilles' is inscribed. A fragment, 5·2 cm high, of an Athenian black-figured mixing bowl, first half of the sixth century B.C.

United Kingdom or Italy, no more than treble that of the state of California.

The Romans had neither the resources nor the interest to bring about a cultural unification of their empire, so that it was permanently divided, in this respect, between the western, Latin half and the eastern, Greek half (which always included Sicily). Games of the Greek type never caught on in the Latin world. The fact that major Games were styled 'world Games', no longer merely 'pan-Hellenic', is misleading. Although a few became a feature of popular entertainment in Italy, notably in the city of Rome itself, the competitors were drawn solely from the Greek half of the empire. And that of course remained true of the numerous and flourishing games in the Greek provinces, including the Olympic Games, despite some attention by the emperors,* by an occasional Roman aristocrat and by Romans who migrated to the eastern provinces and became more or less Hellenized.

The Greek cities had lost their ancient political autonomy, but not their hold on the imagination and pride of their citizens. An Olympic victor in the third century A.D. still identified himself with his city, as had his predecessors a thousand years before, and his city with·him. Municipal affairs, now restricted to education and religion, public works, games and festivals, were in the hands of a minority of wealthy aristocrats (using the word loosely). The latter not only administered these activities but also contributed substantially to the costs. The city officials in charge of games and gymnasia, as we shall see, ranked among the most honoured citizens; they were the successors in the Greek cities of the Roman Empire of the statesmen and generals of the autonomous city-states of a bygone era.

To capture in a short space the long history of the Olympic Games against such a varied and changing background would be difficult enough, without the handicap of inadequate and fragmentary documentation. We rely on a curious miscellany of evidence, among which archaeological finds, figured monuments and paintings on fine pottery

* See Chapter 8.

[11]

are as important as written sources. During the first century or two of the Games, no systematic written records were kept. At the end of the fifth century B.C., a philosopher and rhetorician, Hippias of Elis, collected the information and published a list of Olympic victors, which was revised and corrected by Aristotle a century later. By then, Olympia itself had its own reliable archives, but they have not survived, any more than the lists of Hippias and Aristotle. However, later ancient writers made frequent use of that information, and it is from their works that modern experts have been able to compile a substantial, though incomplete, catalogue of Olympic victors, often with the exact dates. The details of the earliest years are not very reliable, and sometimes certainly apocryphal, but at least we can be grateful to the ancient scholars for providing the essential backbone of knowledge from the date which, they were firmly agreed, marked the institution of the Olympic Games, 776 B.C.

The next body of evidence consists of the athletic scenes painted on fine Athenian pottery, from the middle of the seventh century B.C. to the end of the fourth.* Then, from about the middle of the sixth century B.C. to the end of the fifth, some of the wealthiest victors commissioned odes to be sung chorally at the victory celebrations. Sicilian tyrants, such as Hiero of Syracuse and Theron of Acragas, indulged particularly, but so did private individuals from Athens, Rhodes, Cyrene, Himera in Sicily and many other places. And, what is of the utmost importance, the poets they turned to were among the greatest in the entire history of Greek literature, Simonides of Ceos, his nephew Bacchylides, and above all Pindar of Thebes (Plate 2a), whose probable dates are 518-438 B.C. Of Pindar's large output, hymns and odes of all kinds, forty-five odes for Games victors still

---

* The fact that this evidence is almost exclusively Athenian is a sign not of a particular fondness for games among the Athenians, but of their virtual monopoly in pottery with 'narrative' scenes, which they exported all over Hellas and also to the Etruscans. Games and athletics were by no means the most common subjects. We cannot explain the Athenian monopoly any more than we know the reason for the rather abrupt disappearance of the Greek taste for such pottery at the end of the fourth century B.C.

survive, not because they were about sports but because of the quality of the poetry, rich in imagery, complex in versification and contents, constantly varied in metre and in length (extending once to 300 lines).

After the odes and the painted pottery came to an end, there is a long blank period, with only scraps of information, an occasional remark by a historian or a lucky find of a victor's epigram or a local decree on stone, until it became customary, in the second century B.C., for the more famous athletes to summarize their successes, boastfully and with varied accuracy, on stone or metal plaques or on the bases of their statues, many of which have been discovered by archaeologists (Plate 2b). Finally, there appeared the world's first guide-book, written by Pausanias, who visited Olympia between A.D. 160 and 170, provided a detailed, reliable description of many of its buildings and monuments, and also recorded a fair number of notable incidents in the long history of the Games.

Thereafter the information is reduced to a trickle. We do not even know whether or not the Games continued with regularity after 261 or the precise date when they were finally stopped. An edict of the Christian emperor Theodosius I in 393 ordered that all pagan cults and centres be closed. That was followed at Olympia almost immediately by the conversion of one of the more suitable buildings into a Christian church, and it is unthinkable that the Games were permitted to coexist with a Christian community and Christian worship. By then, the site was half a ruin anyway, thanks to increasing impoverishment and neglect, to a hit-and-run raid by Germanic invaders, the Heruli, late in the third century, followed by an earthquake in about 300. Another, more severe earthquake in the sixth century, then Slavonic invasions effectively put an end to Olympia as a place of habitation. The two nearby rivers completed the process, converting the area into a malarial swamp.

A century-by-century narrative is thus clearly impossible. Visible gaps and uncertainties recur throughout the account. Yet the overall picture, of the competition itself, of the participants and their cities, of their ambitions and their values, is full and rich.

2

Games and Festivals

Olympia lies in a hollow between gentle hills in the district of Elis. The whole region is a fertile one, as any visitor can still observe when coming by road from Patras or, even more strikingly, through the passes of the barren Arcadian mountains to the east. The terrain is gentle, with plains and lovely green hills, lacking the rugged mountains characteristic of most of Greece. It is even more unusual by Greek standards in that it has some rainfall throughout the year, so that the two main rivers, the Peneus in the north and the Alpheus, with its tributaries, which flows through Olympia, do not dry up in the summer.

Evidence of human habitation has been found at Olympia dating earlier than 1500 B.C. About 1000 B.C. the site became a shrine of the god Zeus. Since Zeus had his home on the highest mountain in Greece, Mount Olympus rising to more than 2900 m on the border between Thessaly and Macedon, he became known as Zeus Olympios, and his precinct beside the Alpheus River in Elis was called Olympia. Why that particular spot was chosen, or why it became the most important centre in the whole of Hellas for the worship of Zeus, is unknown; ancient writers, looking back, could offer nothing more than a number of incompatible legendary explanations. What matters, however, is that Olympia throughout its history remained a sacred precinct and nothing else. It never developed into a proper community, let alone a city-state, but was controlled, as we shall see, first by the neighbouring Pisatans and then by the city of Elis (a single city within the district of the same name) on the Peneus River about 40 km to the northwest.

The Olympic Games were founded in 776 B.C. because Olympia was already an established sacred site, not the other way round. In consequence, religious ceremonies occupied a substantial part of the five-day period of the Games, the normal duration once the Games had achieved their classical organization early in the fifth century B.C. The athletic contests did not begin until the second day. There was much preliminary business to get through on the opening day, as in large-scale festivities in all periods of history—checking qualifications, oath-taking and the like. It was also a day for sightseeing and popular entertainment, and for last-minute practising by the athletes. But, above all, in antiquity it was devoted to worship of the gods, to sacrifices, offerings and prayers both by officials and by the individual athletes. The morning of the third day was reserved for more religious ceremony, culminating in the sacrifice of one hundred oxen on the great altar of Zeus (Plate 3).* And when the programme was completed, on the fifth and final day, with celebrations and a banquet in the Magistrates' House for all the victors, there were renewed sacrifices and thank-offerings.

The modern Olympics also have their rituals, such as processions and even oaths, but the ceremonies, for all their pageantry and solemnity, are secular, whereas the ancient ones were religious in the strict sense. The competitors, their male kinsmen and their trainers swore by Zeus that they would obey the rules and play fair, and Zeus was a terrible, avenging god when perjury was involved, with lightning and the thunderbolt at his command (Plate 6b). The fines paid for breaking the rules were spent to erect statues to Zeus (Plate 7a), as a

* For the location of altars, temples and other places within the precinct, see Figs. 7-10.

[15]

permanently visible warning to potential malefactors but also as an appeasement of the great deity. Nor was the pervasive religious tone restricted to the earliest, more primitive (or, at least, less sophisticated) age. Under the Roman Empire athletes were still praying to Zeus for 'either the wreath or death' and counting on the assistance of their patron deity Heracles (more familiarly known to us by his Latin name Hercules). No wonder that after the Empire became Christian, the emperors found the Games intolerable and closed them down.

Probably nothing is harder for a twentieth-century westerner to grasp, at least beneath the surface, than the operations of a polytheistic religion. The Greeks had many gods and goddesses, including such lesser divinities as nymphs and 'heroes', the latter being mortals who had then gained deification, Heracles most notably for our purposes (Plate 6c). There was a hierarchy in divine as in human society. But, though Zeus (Plates 6a, b, 10a) was their king and their superior, each god or goddess was a divine being in his or her own right, immortal, capable of superhuman feats of all sorts, and involved in one or another way in the affairs of man and his environment. Therefore man had to establish a correct relationship with them all, individually and collectively. Otherwise calamities were in store—crop failures, drought, shipwreck, defeat in war, sterility, failure in love.

Obviously no individual or community could find the time or resources to appease or celebrate every divine being on a regular, continuing basis. The gods were not so unreasonable as to demand that, and one way to introduce a measure of order, of system, into the proceedings was to acknowledge a divine division of labour. Like men, individual gods and goddesses had particular functions; so one appealed to Artemis if one went hunting, to Poseidon if one sailed the seas, to Aphrodite (whom the Romans called Venus) for aid in matters of love. Then, since individual gods were patrons of individual cities, the hunter or lover or athlete sought their assistance at the same time. Unfortunately, that simple logic did not prevail through the centuries. Some of the most powerful gods accumulated

functions, such as Apollo in music, soothsaying and healing. Others
shared, and sometimes competed, in functions. That complication
was acknowledged by adding appropriate epithets to the god's name:
at Olympia there was one shrine for Zeus Olympios, another for Zeus
Horkios, to whom the oaths (*horkoi* in Greek) were sworn.

The gods were also not unreasonably jealous. Provided they were
themselves not neglected, they did not mind a measure of sharing with
appropriate colleagues. Zeus could have no possible objection to the
erection at Olympia, quite early, of a temple of Pelops, a local 'hero'
from whom the Peloponnese, the peninsula which constitutes the
southern part of Greece, took its name. If it is less obvious why Hera,
Zeus' consort, should have received the first monumental temple
(Plates 6d, 8a), before Zeus himself, that is only because we are too
ignorant of the prehistory and early history of the shrine to grasp the
reason.

Within one of the earlier secular buildings, the Magistrates' House,
stood a shrine of the goddess Hestia (literally 'the Hearth'), precisely
as in every private house throughout the Greek world. And that
reveals another essential point: the ancient world never knew anything
like the modern idea of a separation between church and state. One
of the community's main functions, along with food supply and
defence, was the regular and proper performance of a variety of
religious duties, complementary to, not in place of, the rituals per-
formed by individuals. Religious festivals, therefore, such as the
Olympic Games, were official public activities, the responsibility of
the controlling community through special functionaries who were
normally laymen, not priests. That is to say, though there were
officials called 'priests', they were in most instances not men in holy
orders, with a vocation and special training, but laymen (in our sense)
who had been selected to take charge of sacred rites in the same way
as others were selected for secular functions. The government also
determined who participated in Games, whether as performers or
even as spectators. At Olympia, for instance, women were excluded
altogether.

So much control over religion was potentially a powerful weapon in the hands of a state, but it was tempered by the fact that the concern was largely with externals, with rituals rather than with beliefs or dogmas. Every community promulgated sacred laws in large numbers, detailed prescriptions defining, for example, who was to sacrifice what, when, and under what conditions, and so on. The individual's inner feelings were his own affair, provided he did not openly blaspheme or deny the existence of the gods or otherwise risk bringing divine retribution on his neighbours and on the whole community. In a treatise on piety, Aristotle's pupil, the philosopher Theophrastus, summed up the traditional attitude in this way: one sacrificed either to honour the gods or to thank them or to beg a favour. When he wrote that, he in effect summed up what went on at Olympia, on the part of officials and participants.

For all their immortality and superhuman potency, the gods had their material side: they ate and drank, made love, quarrelled and enjoyed luxuries. Hence one way to honour and placate them was to share goods with them: sacrifices and libations, the first fruits of the harvest, a proportion of the spoils of war, gifts of all kinds. Temples, the earthly homes of the gods, thus became treasure-houses, and the great pan-Hellenic sanctuaries naturally exceeded the purely local shrines in this respect. Ancient Olympia must have been a remarkable place to visit, packed indoors and out with offerings from both individuals and communities, ranging from small tokens to expensive bronze *objets d'art* and life-size statues, again usually in bronze, of victorious athletes (Plates IIa, 7). On a terrace overlooking the sacred precinct there were even a dozen 'treasure-houses' in a row, each built by a different Greek city, with its name over the entrance (Plate 7a). Today it is difficult to visualize the clutter, for not only are the buildings in ruins but the large statues and treasures have long disappeared. The Romans pilfered many to add to their private art collections, the barbarian invaders of the late Empire destroyed others, and the local population completed the destruction during the Middle Ages, using the stone and metal for their houses, fences and other mundane purposes. At the end of the second century A.D., however, Pausanias listed nearly two hundred large statues he had seen, still in place.

It was consonant with the earthy, one might almost say merry, side of Greek religion that the chief occasion for celebrating a particular divinity was commonly a festival. There were many hundreds, perhaps even thousands, every year in the scattered Greek world, varying greatly in their scale and pomp, in the extent to which they were purely local or achieved pan-Hellenic status, and in their programmes. They all included the elements of worship, processions, sacrifices and prayers; normally they also included a feast, and quite commonly competitions in choral music, dancing, the drama and sports (but never in the practical arts), in different combinations. Olympia's exclusive concentration on sports, at least in the official programme, was uncommon. Early in the Roman Empire, oratorical contests featuring encomia of the Roman emperor, or of the chief god or gods of the host-city, were introduced into the Pythian, Isthmian and Panathenaic Games, among many others. But they were not allowed to encroach at Olympia. That is perhaps the neatest symbol of the unique standing of the Olympic Games.

The origins of the Greek passion for competitive games is lost in the obscurity of prehistory. The earliest, and most famous, account appears in the earliest work of Greek literature to survive, Homer's *Iliad*, which narrates at length the games Achilles organized to accompany the burial rites of his comrade Patroclus, killed by Hector in individual combat before the gates of Troy. The competitors were drawn exclusively from the princely leaders of the Greek forces (Plates IIb, 9a); the events included a two-horse chariot race, a foot race, boxing, wrestling and weight throwing; the prizes which Achilles provided for the winners were not wreaths or other tokens but expensive treasures, such as bronze cauldrons and tripods (Plate 7c), horses and captive women. The games in the *Iliad* thus reveal that as far back as our evidence goes the Greeks did not draw the line between the sacred and the secular where we do; that the competitive element was essential; that noblemen were also sportsmen, eager to contest with each other and not in the least reluctant to receive the equivalent of large cash prizes.

There was no inconsistency between worship and fiercely competitive games as parts of a single religious celebration. One respected the gods, feared them, acknowledged dependence on them and gratitude to them. But one rarely loved them or humbled oneself. Meekness and humility never became ranking virtues in the pagan world. Success might be assisted by divine favour and it could certainly be hampered by divine disfavour, but application, hard work and self-reliance were the key and a man then had a right to be proud of his personal achievement. An Olympic victor could dedicate a small statue inscribed 'I belong to Zeus' (Plate 9b) without throwing the smallest shadow on his own talents, his own efforts, his own virtues. That was repeatedly stressed in the victory odes, for example in the following lines of Pindar:

> For if any man delights in expense and toil
> And sets in action high gifts shaped by the gods,
> And with him his destiny
> Plants the glory which he desires,
> Already he casts his anchor on the furthest edge of bliss,
> And the gods honour him.

The gods, in other words, were patrons of success rather than its creators. And so, too, with fair play and ethical behaviour. The Greek gods issued no Ten Commandments. When an Olympic athlete swore by Zeus Horkios on the first day of the Games, he promised to obey the man-made rules of the games. The god's role was as patron of justice, and the punisher of injustice, but again not as the creator. Zeus Horkios was the externalized form of what we call 'conscience'.

Victory alone brought glory: participation, games-playing for its own sake, was no virtue; defeat brought undying shame. Again Pindar gives us the tone, in an ode in honour of a young wrestler:

And now four times you came down with bodies beneath you
(You meant them harm),
To whom the Pythian feast has given
No glad homecoming like yours.
They, when they meet their mothers,
Have no sweet laughter around them moving delight.
In back streets out of their enemies' way
They cower; disaster has bitten them.

That helps explain why competitors prayed for 'either the wreath or death'.

Greek (and Roman) society was shot through with the competitive spirit. The normal Greek word for an athletic contest was *agon*, which could be used for any contest or struggle (hence our word 'agony'), such as a battle or a lawsuit, as well as for games. Choruses and playwrights competed, as did runners or wrestlers. Ambition, in Greek *philotimia* (literally 'love of honour'), was always praiseworthy, in public affairs as in private. When the Greek historian Herodotus visited Egypt he was astonished to find no organized games. He should not have been surprised: open competition in games is incompatible with such rigidly stratified societies as those of the ancient Near East, with their Pharaohs and other absolute monarchs at the apex, divinely sanctioned and sometimes gods themselves.

The roots of the Greek competitive spirit go back to the time of the Homeric poems, when Achilles, Agamemnon, Odysseus and the other noble warriors were, in the poet's words, 'athletes, not merchants', who openly expressed the wish 'always to be the first and to surpass the others'; when old Nestor could say proudly of his son Antilochus that he was 'the fastest runner and a warrior'. Those were days when individual combat still played a large part in warfare as in games. What is remarkable is the tenacity with which the old values survived after the armies became citizen militias fighting in formation (the hoplite phalanx), later a fully professional soldiery. Athletes continued to be praised, by poets and by themselves, for their courage (*andreia*, literally 'manliness'); comparisons continued to be drawn between athletics and war, and in the glory to be gained from both.

'Always to be first and to surpass the others' must be understood literally and strictly. There was no second place or third place, no silver or bronze medal; not to be first was to lose and that was all there was to it. Nor did it much matter whether one won in a walkover (Plate 15b) or with a poor throw or in slow time. Records in that sense were never kept: there was no way even to say in Greek 'to set a record' or 'to break a record'. The common modern explanation that running records are impossible without watches seems inadequate: the Greeks were perfectly capable of measuring the distance of a jump or a discus throw. Instead, they kept other kinds of records, and were quick to boast about them, for example, the number of victories a man won during his career or the fact that he was never brought to his knees in a wrestling-match.

There were rare exceptions to the first-only rule, notably in the pentathlon, and there was one general, significant exception beyond that: in the horse and chariot races, in which the owner was the winner, not the rider, men of unusual wealth sometimes entered several horses or chariots in the same race. Then they could be proud of gaining second, and even fourth, place, *but only if they were also first*. Otherwise the competition in games was strictly an individual affair. Team games were never introduced, and apparently never considered. Glory could not be shared with partners, but only, after the event, with one's family and ancestors and with one's city.

Olympia itself, as we have already seen, was neither a city nor a community. Indeed, the whole district of Elis remained throughout antiquity an underdeveloped agrarian region with little urbanization: not until 472 B.C. was the city-state of Elis created, by a voluntary amalgamation of several villages. How then, we are bound to wonder, did a festival in this backwater rise to preeminence? Part of the answer, though not the complete answer (which we shall never know), lies precisely in the unimportance of Elis. Games everywhere were managed by local authorities, not by an international committee, and the weaker that authority the less the risk that the prestige of a great festival would enhance its political power. Athletes from all over the Greek world could safely compete for their own glory and that of their own cities, without building up the prestige of a powerful host-community.

Although in the early period the Eleans engaged in petty local wars with their neighbours, once they had subjugated the area in and around Olympia and won control of the Games from the Pisatans in about 570 B.C., they showed little ambition, or capacity, for fighting wars. They could not remain completely neutral in the various Greek power struggles around them, between Athens and Sparta, for example, or later, after Alexander the Great, between Sparta, the Achaean League and the kings of Macedonia. Nor could they always prevent invasions, as by Sparta in 400 B.C., in punishment for their having sided with Athens, or by neighbouring Arcadia in 365 and again in 364 B.C. when fighting reached the precinct itself on the second day of the Games, interrupting the pentathlon. But on the whole the Eleans managed to avoid fighting, as distinct from declaring an allegiance, and, when they were defeated, they had the final protection that they were a 'sacred people' responsible for 'the honours due to the gods'. That function, said the fourth-century B.C. historian Xenophon, could not be entrusted to the rustic population in the immediate vicinity of Olympia.

Long before the Spartan and Arcadian invasions, the Olympic Games had achieved their place, which they never lost, at the pinnacle of all the pan-Hellenic games. By the middle of the sixth century B.C., the 'big four' were firmly established as such: the Greek word for them was *periodos*, literally 'the Circuit' (as we shall refer to them hereafter). The Olympic Games and the Pythian at Delphi (in honour of Apollo) were quadrennial, the other two biennial, the Nemean at Nemea on the northern boundary of the Argolid in the Peloponnese, also in honour of Zeus, and the Isthmian at Corinth, at a festival of Poseidon (Plates 18, 19). Despite the absence of a central Greek political or ecclesiastical authority, the Circuit was so arranged that at least one of the Games was held in every year. In an Olympic year, outstanding athletes could compete in the Isthmian Games as well, the following year at the Nemean, then in both the Pythian and the Isthmian, and in the fourth year at Nemea again.

All four offered only wreaths as prizes, the Pythian Games a laurel wreath (from which we get our 'laurels'), the Isthmian one of pine-branches, the Nemean a crown of wild celery (Plates 10a, b). The Olympic wreath was fashioned from the branches of a sacred olive-tree growing within the precinct, and presumably the prize had a magical value, at least in the early days. Three of the Games were managed locally, but the Pythian was complicated by the existence from very early times of a council of cities connected with the oracle of Apollo at Delphi. The troubles which ensued, when individual member-states of the council sought to gain control of Delphi and its treasures, proved the inadvisability of linking prestigious games with political power.

The long continuance in the Circuit of token prizes had nothing to do with amateurism or with aristocratic origins. Olympic winners were well rewarded by their native cities, and genuinely professional athletes were free to participate on an absolutely equal footing with tyrants and aristocrats. As the years rolled on, more and more so-called 'prize games' were introduced, with substantial monetary awards, the number eventually exceeding three hundred. These were local affairs to honour a local deity or 'hero', or annual memorial festivals for a deceased benefactor. New 'sacred games' came into being, too, especially in the centuries after Alexander the Great. Eventually, Roman emperors sanctioned, and sometimes initiated, new games in several eastern cities which were called 'Olympic'. Neither that curious practice nor anything else dislodged the original, true Olympic Games from their pinnacle until the day when they were closed down permanently.

As the Greek world underwent changes, both political and economic, the participants came from different social classes and from different regions. At first they were chiefly from Elis itself and neighbouring districts: from 776 to 600 B.C. the Peloponnese provided some 75 per cent of the victors. Then athletes from the whole Greek mainland and from the western settlements began to enter in substantial numbers. In Roman times, the number of winners from the mainland of Greece declined to perhaps 10 per cent of the total, whereas Asia Minor produced some 60 per cent. However, such figures merely mean that Asia Minor had displaced other, less prosperous parts of Hellas as the home of champions, and probably produced more athletes altogether.*

The Pindaric ode already quoted about 'expense and toil' was composed to celebrate the victory of a boy from the little island of Aegina at the Isthmian Games. His father had been a Nemean winner, and now the poet looked ahead to still greater glory for the family:

> May a third time come
> To make preparations for the Olympian Saviour on Aegina
> And pour offerings of honey-voiced hymns.

An Olympic olive wreath was the crowning ambition of every athlete, whether in the fifth century B.C. or in the third century A.D.

* We have no way of estimating the number of competitors from the different regions, apart from the victors.

3

The Olympic Programme

In the spring of an Olympic year, three 'sacred heralds' set out from Olympia to visit every corner of Hellas, proclaiming the forthcoming Games. The date was fixed according to a complicated religious calendar, so that the third day of the Games always coincided with either the second or the third full moon after the summer solstice. The competitors were required to arrive in Elis at least one month beforehand and to train under the supervision of the judges. Others, by the tens of thousands, came as, when and how they chose—spectators, food and drink purveyors, official representatives of many Greek cities (normally bearing gifts to Zeus), touts and gamblers and pimps with strings of girls (who plied their trade outside the sacred precinct since it was closed to women), pedlars, flower-sellers, and the singers, dancers and orators who provided the 'fringe' programme —in short, the sort of motley assemblage found at great fairs everywhere or, still in our time, at certain shrines on the more popular holy days, such as Assumption Day on the Greek island of Tenos.

A first-century A.D. picture of the 'fringe' at the Isthmian Games as Diogenes was supposed to have seen it four centuries earlier, though nastily satirical in tone, may give some idea of the reality:

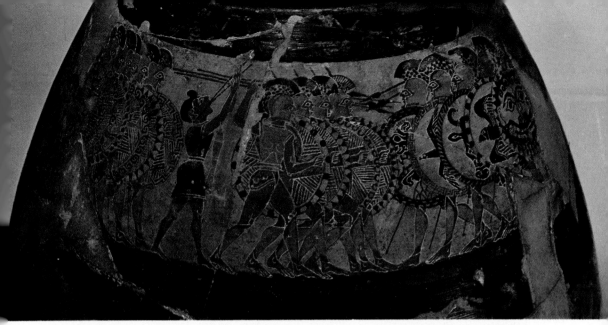

PLATE III (a) The hoplite formation in action — one of the earliest representations, painted about 640 B.C., of the then fairly new phalanx of heavily armed infantrymen. The full hoplite panoply is clearly portrayed, as well as the thrusting spear, different in size (and in the way it is held) from the javelin used in the Games. The hoplites advanced to the music of the flute player. This is a portion of the upper frieze, about 5 cm high, of a tall Corinthian jug, known as the 'Chigi Vase', now in the Villa Giulia in Rome.

(b) The race in armour. In addition to the four competitors, each carrying a shield with a richly decorated personal blazon, there are two spectators, and, at each side, cauldrons on tripods which had become a conventional symbol on vase paintings of Games prizes (see Plate 7c). The picture is on a 35·8 cm Athenian black-figured 'neck amphora' of the middle of the sixth century B.C., twenty or thirty years before this race was added to the Olympic Games, and at a time when the competitors in this event still wore greaves (see Fig. 6).

PLATE IV The four-horse chariot is shown at full speed about to round the turning-post. In the *Iliad* Nestor advises his son '. . . make your left-hand horse keep hard against the turning post . . .' (see p. 30). A Panathenaic amphora (see p. 56 and the note to Plate Va) of the late fifth century B.C., found in Cyrene in North Africa, awarded to the winner in a chariot race. Like the amphoras in Plates VIIb, 21, this one retained the black-figured technique long after it had been abandoned in favour of red figure on other Athenian pottery.

Many miserable sophists could be heard shouting and reviling each other round the temple of Poseidon while their so-called pupils fought with one another. Writers were reading their rubbish aloud. Many poets were reciting their verses to the applause of others, many conjurers were showing off their tricks, fortune-tellers theirs. There were countless advocates perverting the law and not a few pedlars hawking everything and anything.

At Olympia, the chariot race was the opening event after the initial day of preparation and worship.* The two-wheeled chariots, each drawn by four horses abreast (Plate IV), entered the Hippodrome in a procession headed by the purple-robed judges, a herald and a trumpeter. As the competitors passed the judges' stand, the herald called out the names of the owner, his father and his city. Then he proclaimed the Games officially open, with the most spectacular (as well as the most costly) of all the events. To us that may appear bad planning, for the chariot-race seems perfect for the climax rather than the beginning of the Games. The idea seems to have been to open with the competition that offered the greatest opportunity for pomp and splendour, and no subsequent entry parade or contest was comparable on that score.

The Hippodrome was not a building but a large, rectangular, more or less flat, open space immediately to the southeast of the Stadium (see Figs. 7-10). The northern side was closed off by a low hill, on which spectators stood, the southern side by an artificial embankment, also for spectators. There were seats only for the judges and a few celebrities. The course was marked by the starting-line and two turning-posts at either end, with neither a barrier between the down and up lanes nor a curved track. The starting-line was more

---

* No ancient authority reports the actual sequence of events. The one we have adopted is perhaps the most plausible one, in so far as the evidence goes, and it refers to the classical five-day Games after they were reorganized in 472 B.C. There were changes in the hundreds of years that followed, but they cannot be traced with any accuracy.

[27]

than 250 metres wide, and the distance between the posts was probably a little short of 400 metres.

We do not know the size of the entry in an Olympic chariot race:
the largest number on record in any Greek contest is forty-one, at
the Pythian Games of 462 B.C. when the race was won by Arcesilas,
king of Cyrene in northern Africa, whose chariot was the only one to
complete the course. Even half that number on the Olympic ground
challenges the most imaginative 'Hollywood epic' director, and we
are not helped in our reconstruction by the fact that over the centuries
the river has washed away all traces of the ancient Hippodrome.

Once the chariots and horses were lined up, a difficult and time-
consuming operation, the problem was to compensate those at the
ends, who had to cover a greater distance in order to reach the far
turning-post the first time. (Positions on the starting-line were
assigned by lot.) The solution eventually arrived at was a staggered

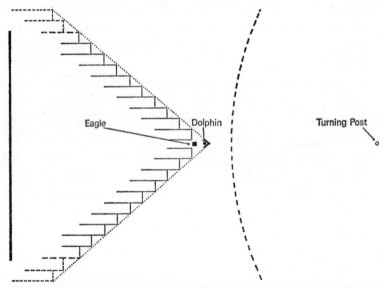

Fig. 1 The starting-gate for the Olympic chariot race, a reconstruction based on the description by Pausanias summarized in the text.
The turning-post shown in the figure is the one nearest the start. The
other turning-post was perhaps 400 metres to the right.

[28]

start controlled by a simple mechanical device. A long starting-gate was fashioned, shaped like the prow of a ship, according to Pausanias, with separate stalls for each chariot (Fig. 1). A cranking-device at the centre raised the gates in sequence, beginning with those at the outer ends and steadily working towards the centre, so that those with the greatest distance to run had the advantage of speed by the time all the chariots were in motion on a slightly concave line. For the benefit of the spectators, the trumpeter signalled both the beginning and the end of the manœuvres with the gates, a bronze dolphin perched on a pole at the centre of the 'prow' came down while a bronze eagle 'flew' from an altar. 'From then on', Pausanias continues, 'it is all a matter of the skill of the drivers and the speed of the horses.'

A flatter understatement is hard to imagine. For twelve laps, more than 9 kilometres, the flying horses pulled the light carts in short bursts of speed punctuated by 180-degree turns at the posts. Although the rules forbade swerving in front of a competitor, bumps, crashes and head-on collisions were the rule rather than the exception, as chariots raced up and down the narrow unseparated course and made one wide turn after another. Arcesilas' victory as the lone finisher was not normal, but it is not very surprising.

In the most beautifully and precisely observed description of its kind from the whole of ancient Greek literature, Homer's account of the funeral games for Patroclus, old Nestor gives his son the following advice on how to compensate for the known slowness of his horses:

> It is by skill that the sea captain holds his rapid ship
> on its course, though torn by winds, over the wine-blue water.
> By skill charioteer outpasses charioteer. He
> who has put all his confidence in his horses and chariot
> and recklessly makes a turn that is loose one way or another
> finds his horses drifting out of the course and does not control
> them . . .
>
> You must drive your chariot and horses so as to hug this [the
> turning-post],

and yourself, in the strong-fabricated chariot, lean over
a little to the left of the course, and as for your right horse,
            whip him
and urge him along, slackening your hands to give him his full
            rein,
but make your left-hand horse keep hard against the turning-post
so that the hub's edge of your fashioned wheel will seem to be
touching it, yet take care not really to brush against it,
for, if so, you might damage your horses and break your chariot,
and that will be a thing of joy for the others, and a failure
for you. So, dear son, drive thoughtfully and be watchful.
For if you follow the others but get first by the turning-post,
there is none who could sprint to make it up, nor close you, nor
            pass you.

The excitement among the spectators must have mounted to a wild crescendo when the trumpet's blare announced the last half-lap, a straight gallop to the finishing-post. The judges presented the victorious owner with his olive wreath (Plate 23a); he was acclaimed by loud shouts and pelted with flowers and branches. The charioteers, whose skill and courage were decisive, remained curiously shadowy figures, never achieving anything comparable to the frenzied popularity of Roman and Byzantine jockeys and charioteers. Like the managers of the stud farms where the winning horses were bred, they were merely part of the necessary but unsung underpinning of the contest, even when they were enshrined in a statue commemorating the owner's victory (Plate IIa).

The chariot had for many centuries ceased to be a functional vehicle, whether for transport or in war. But in the Homeric funeral games, at least, the noble princes themselves were the drivers in the races; now the chariots had become pure status symbols, the charioteers mere hirelings of the wealthy aristocratic owners. An interesting by-product was the opportunity for women to 'win' an Olympic event without desecrating the Games by their physical presence. The first was Cynisca, daughter of King Agesilaus II of Sparta, who won the chariot race twice, in 396 and 392 B.C., and made splendid dedications to Zeus in commemoration. Others followed on infrequent occasions, the last apparently a lady from Elis itself in the mid-second century A.D., in a late and relatively minor event, the race for chariots drawn by colts.

Horse racing developed along parallel lines. Although, as we have seen, cavalry units had become of secondary importance in Greek armies, service in them was still honorific, and every landed gentleman had his stables and rode his horses—but not in the races at the great Games. Again the anonymous jockey won the honours for the owner.

The Olympic horse race followed in the Hippodrome immediately after the chariot race, on the same course. No wonder gentlemen preferred not to ride themselves: riding an unshod horse bareback and without stirrups (neither the horse-shoe nor the stirrup was known in antiquity) over a field that had just been churned up by the chariot-teams could not have been much fun (Plate 11b). 'Horse-back riding of a strenuous sort', wrote Galen the Greek physician from Pergamum, late in the second century A.D., 'has been known to rupture parts in the region of the kidneys, and has often brought injuries to the chest or sometimes to the spermatic passages—to say nothing of the missteps of the horses, because of which riders have often been pitched from their seat and instantly killed.'

The Olympic horse race also required a fanned out line of horses to head for the far turning-post and then back, apparently for only a single lap, about 800 metres. Pausanias tells an old story which illuminates the situation, at least with respect to the poor jockey and how little he counted for.

The mare of Phidolas of Corinth [he writes] is called Breeze according to the Corinthian records, and just as the race started she threw her rider, yet she ran just as perfectly, turned round the post, and when she heard the trumpet quickened her pace and got to the judges first; she realized she had won and stood still. The Eleans proclaimed Phidolas the winner and allowed him to dedicate his mare.

His sons, continuing the tradition, won at the Isthmian Games and at the Olympic Games of 508 B.C. with a horse called Wolf.

The afternoon of the second day was devoted to the pentathlon, held in the Stadium with the probable exception of the wrestling, which was apparently contested in the open spaces round the altar of Zeus. The ground was prepared for these events, and for all that followed to the close of the Games, by being broken up with a pick-axe and then covered with a thick layer of sand. (A pick-axe is occasionally included in Games pictures, as in Plate 14.) From late in the sixth century B.C., furthermore, all contestants were naked and barefoot as they raced, jumped or wrestled on the sand—a Spartan innovation, according to the historian Thucydides, writing at the end of the fifth century B.C.

The first three events of the pentathlon, the discus, the standing long jump and the javelin, were restricted to the pentathlon, whereas the 200-metre sprint and wrestling were also independent events on the fourth day (Plate Va). The discus, usually of bronze, was shaped the same as ours and thrown in much the same way, though it was probably somewhat heavier (Plates 13, 23d). Each competitor was given five throws, only his best counting, marked out by a peg (Fig. 2). The same rule applied to the javelin event, in which the missile, lighter and longer than the hoplite's thrusting-spear (Plate IIIa), was norm-ally blunted at the end and was hurled with the aid of a thong. A cord, 30-45 cm in length, was wound tightly round the shaft near the centre of gravity, leaving a loop of 7-10 cm which was grasped by one finger (Fig. 3 and Plates VI, 14). The effect was both to give the arm additional leverage and to impart a spin to the javelin in flight, thereby helping it to retain its direction and to carry much farther. Experi-ments in the nineteenth century, one of them sponsored by Napoleon, suggested that, after sufficient practice, a thrower might more than double the distance.

Fig. 2 Marking the discus throw (from an Athenian cup, about 525 B.C.).

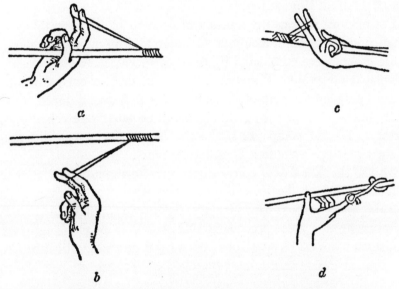

Fig. 3 Illustrations of the finger-thong used in throwing the javelin (see also Plates VI, 14): (a), (b) and (c) are copied from Greek vases, but (d) is modern, from New Caledonia.

That is simple enough, but the long jump presents a confused picture. The jumpers carried a pair of stone or metal weights of varied shapes (some look very much like dumb-bells), with an average

[33]

weight among surviving specimens of two kilogrammes (Plate 15b). They were swung forwards to shoulder height, and then, on the down swing, the jumper leaned well forward and leaped as the weights came down to his knees (Plate 15a). The purpose, we are told by ancient writers, was a dual one, to increase the length of the jump and to assure a clean landing, without which the jump was ruled a foul. Recent experiments show that both effects are achieved only in a standing jump, which can be increased by as much as 20 cm, whereas weights invariably reduce the length of a running jump. What remains uncertain is whether each contestant was given five separate jumps, as with the discus and javelin, or whether he had to jump five times in a continuous progression, with a single bad landing having the effect of an elimination.*

For obvious reasons the number of entrants in the pentathlon was small, and it was not uncommon for some to drop out along the way, while others were eliminated by their performance. Victory was not calculated on points. If anyone was first in three events, that automatically ended the contest. Otherwise the field was reduced for the final contest, the wrestling (in which three falls were required for victory), to those competitors who still had a chance to win because of their placing in the four completed events.

And so the first day of competition came to an end. The following day, the third of the festival, coincided with the full moon. The morning was occupied with various religious rites, public and private, culminating in a great procession that started from the Magistrates' House and wound its way about the sacred precinct until it reached the altar of Zeus. At the head marched the judges, followed by the priests in charge of the sacrifice, the 'sacred embassies' from many cities (bearing costly gifts to the patron god), the athletes, their kinsmen and trainers. Arriving at the altar, they watched the final act. One hundred oxen were slain on the large platform, and their thighs were burned (Plate 3b) on the mound of ashes that had accumulated

* The Greeks never introduced high jumping or hurdling into their games, nor did they jump horses competitively.

above, which were never removed because they were sacred to the god—Pausanias reports that in his day the mound was 6·5 metres high. The rest of the flesh was removed to the Magistrates' House, where it was consumed in the concluding banquet.

The afternoon was given over to the three boys' events (we should say 'juniors'), the 200-metre race, wrestling and boxing. A 'boy' was defined at Olympia as anyone who had passed his twelfth birthday but had not reached his eighteenth, when military service normally began in Greek city-states. Predictably, such a crude classification opened a Pandora's box of troubles for the judges in a world without birth certificates, as we shall see in a later chapter. But Olympia, with its typical conservatism, clung to it, whereas more diverse age-classes were introduced at other Games, and some Games in Asia Minor under the Roman Empire even allowed a competitor to enter both boys' and men's events. One wonders just how old Damiscus of Messene (in the Peloponnese) was in fact, when as a 'twelve-year old' he won the sprint in 368 B.C. and was rewarded with a statue that Pausanias was able to see more than five hundred years later. And a wrestling-match between a twelve-year-old and a seventeen-year-old could hardly have been worth the journey to Olympia for either contestants or spectators.

Damiscus' statue, it should be said, was not exceptional. Not only were the boys' events a feature of all Games, but they attracted entrants from all classes of society. One quarter of Pindar's surviving odes were composed in honour of victors from this group, and Pindar's poetic services were expensive. Centuries later, under the Roman Empire, boy winners were still being honoured by their cities along with their seniors (Plate 24a).

The morning of the final day of the competition was fully occupied with the three running events, 200 metres, 400 metres and the long-distance race (4800 metres), all held in the Stadium, a flat area at the foot of the Hill of Cronus (Plate 18a) with an artificial embankment on the other side, much like the Hippodrome. The start was marked by a row of marble sills, spaced off for each runner, who rested his back foot against his sill, kept his other foot a few inches in front and leaned forward for the start (Plate 9b). False starts were punished, and a starting-gate which was introduced in the fifth century B.C. will have helped (Plate 18c).

The sprint was a straight dash down the stadium, the 400-metre race was double the distance, or one full lap, the 4800-metre run twelve laps. That much is clear but little else. Did the sprinters run to posts at the opposite end spaced as the starting-sills were spaced, or did even they have to race for the single turning-post as the runners seem to have done in the longer distances (and as the horses and chariots certainly did)? The latter would have created obvious diffi-

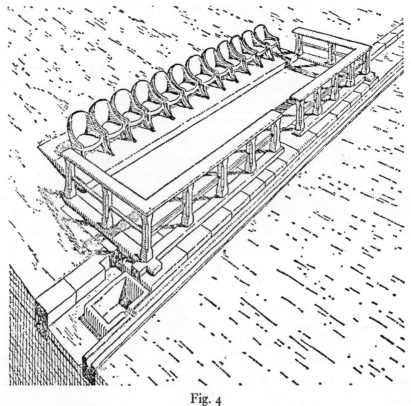

Fig. 4

culties and inequities: the unlucky competitors who drew positions at the wings received no compensation for the greater distance they were compelled to run. Yet, as the judges' stand was not at the end but about one third of the way down the track (Fig. 4 and Plate 18a), it is hard to envisage how they could have settled a photo-finish unless the turning-post was the goal for all. There were rules against tripping and bumping, but ancient writers imply that such tricks were frequent and familiar, again an argument for the turning-post.

A final uncertainty arises from the fact that there was space for only twenty men on the starting-line. Heats were necessary if there were more entrants; in that case, either four or eight runners competed in each heat, with only the winners in the final race. On any count, the interest and the excitement must have been geared to something different from the modern race in clearly marked lanes over precisely equal distances on a proper track. Record times would obviously have been pretty meaningless under such conditions.

At last the moment came, on the final afternoon, for the tough and exceedingly popular body-contact sports, wrestling, boxing and the pankration. The procedure was similar to our own: lots were drawn from a silver urn, the winners in each pair fought each other, and so on, until the final bouts. The draw naturally gave patron deities a chance to extend favours: the element of faith and magic behind Lady Luck explains the otherwise curious practice occasionally noticed of depicting on coins and monuments the urn from which the draw was made (Plates 24a, c).

All three sports were brutal, not to say violent, in varying degrees. There were few rules, no time limits and no ring. There were also no weight-classes, so that top-level competition was restricted to big men, well muscled and tough. Ancient writers disagreed about the relative importance of technique on the one hand and weight and strength on the other, but that seems a rather academic dispute. The many stories about the meat-eating capacity of the great boxers and wrestlers are more to the point, and the representations in paintings and sculpture, including the occasional caricature, stressed muscles and a bull neck (Plates 16, 21). 'Not even Olympian Zeus watched without trembling', says an epigram writer, when Nicophon, 'the Milesian giant' with the thick bull neck, the iron shoulders of Atlas, the hair and beard of Heracles, the eyes of a lion, won the boxing event (in 8 B.C.).

The aim in a wrestling match was to score three falls. A fall was defined as touching the ground with the knees. The half-legendary Milo of Croton, a great meat-eater, warrior and disciple of the philosopher Pythagoras, boasted that he was never brought to his knees: he won the boys' wrestling at Olympia in 540 B.C., the senior event at five successive Olympiads between 532 and 516, as well as six times in the Pythian Games, ten times in the Isthmian and nine

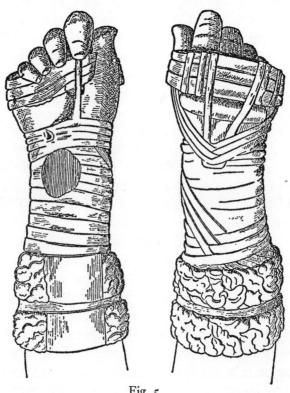

Fig. 5

times in the Nemean. Presumably biting or gouging was prohibited, but not much else (Plate 17). A fifth-century B.C. wrestler named Leontiscus, from Messina in Sicily, tried to break his opponent's fingers as quickly as possible. He was remembered because he was one of the first wrestlers to develop new holds beyond the conventional ones.

Nevertheless, wrestling did not rank as a brutal sport; few stories give it an image of being particularly bloody and painful, let alone of being a cause of death. Boxing was the really tough sport. Leather thongs were wound tightly round the hands and wrists, leaving the fingers free, and the originally soft leather eventually gave way to hard, sharp thongs (Fig. 5). Blows were allowed with both the fist and the open hand; few punches were prohibited. The two contestants fought on, without a break, until one or the other was either knocked out or raised his right hand as a sign of defeat.

No wonder that drawing blood was the least of the damage one might inflict (Plate 20). To have completed a boxing career 'unwounded' (*atraumatistos*) was a rare and understandable boast. Only one man, Cleoxenos of Alexandria, appears with that adjective appended to his name in what survives of the Olympic victor lists (under date of 240 B.C.). Another renowned pugilist, Melancomas in the first century A.D., was able to keep up his guard indefinitely, avoiding blows until his opponent gave up from exhaustion. However, he never won at Olympia. The singularity of his technique kept his name alive, and his unmarked face. In a mocking Greek epigram written in Rome at the time of Nero, the poet Lucillius addressed a fictitious boxer named Stratophon: When Odysseus came home after twenty years, his dog recognized him at once. But you, after a mere four hours' boxing, are unrecognizable not only to dogs but to the city. Look in a mirror and you will say under oath, 'I am not Stratophon.'

There is a story that Cleomedes of Astypalaea (an Aegean island) 'unjustly' killed an opponent at the Games in 492 B.C. The judges denied him his victory and he subsequently went mad. We are not told what rule he had broken, but it was the foul, not the killing, that was punished. Death was one of the recognized risks in sporting competitions; hence the law exempted fatal accidents from a charge of homicide. Another story, repeated by Pausanias, is about two boxers in the Nemean Games, one from Syracuse, the other from Epidamnus, who could not score a knockout and finally agreed to hit each other in turn until one went down or gave up. The first punch was to the head; the counter-punch, to the body, was somehow so contrived as to allow the fingers to penetrate to the entrails and tear them out, causing death. No doubt that is just one of those stories guides have always told to gullible tourists. 'Zeus', prayed an ancient satirist, 'protect me from your guides at Olympia.' But what is revealing about this story is the denouement: the judges disqualified the victor not for a foul but for violating the agreement by administering more than one blow in his turn.

All in all, ancient boxing appears to have been more ferocious than the modern version. Blood was what the spectators came for, and blood was what they got. The classic ancient dream-book, by Artemidorus of Ephesus, explained that to dream of boxing is bad luck for everyone except 'those who handle blood in order to earn a living, namely, doctors, priests in charge of sacrifices, and cooks'. The line between fair and foul play was drawn closer to 'anything goes' than we accept today. It was unknown for boxers (or any athletes for that matter) to shake hands before or after a match. The spirit of Pindar's lines, 'You meant them harm . . . disaster has bitten them', was incompatible with such a gesture.

Then, as if the wrestling and boxing were not enough, the programme continued with the favourite sport of all, the pankration, a technical term created out of the Greek adjective, *pankrates*, 'all-powerful' (applied to Zeus, for example). It can be described as a combination of wrestling and judo, with a bit of boxing thrown in. The common English translation, 'trial of strength', is a polite fiction: the contestants punched, slapped, kicked, wrestled (much of the time on the ground) and even—though illegally—bit and gouged each other until one surrendered by tapping the victor on the back or shoulder (Plate 22).

Predictably, this sport also produced its crop of gory tales. Pausanias tells one about an Arcadian pankratiast who had reached the finals in search of his third Olympic victory. The unnamed opponent 'caught Arrachion, held him with a scissors grip and at the same time throttled him with his hands; so Arrachion broke one of the man's toes. Arrachion died by strangling, and at the same time the strangler gave in from the pain in his toe. The Eleans crowned the dead body of Arrachion with the wreath and proclaimed it as the winner.' And his native city of Phigalia erected his statue in its central square. Then there was Sostratus of Sicyon, winner in the Olympic Games of 364, 360 and 356 B.C., and fourteen times in the rest of the Circuit. He adopted the trick of the wrestler Leontiscus and acquired the nickname of 'Mr Finger-tips' as a reward, also a statue in Delphi, another at Olympia (where Pausanias saw it standing, appropriately enough, alongside the statue of Leontiscus), and his portrait on some of the coins of Sicyon.*

Yet the ancients held the pankration to be less dangerous than boxing. It was widely indulged in, not only by more or less professional athletes but even by boys in the local gymnasia. One can only guess today at this seemingly perverse judgment. One more event remained before the competition was closed, the 400-metre race in armour. A later writer says that it was held last in order to mark the end of the Olympic truce, but that sounds a learned, after the fact explanation without any foundation. The simpler and more plausible explanation is that it was felt desirable to reflect in the Games the fact that the infantry had supplanted the cavalry as the main Greek military arm. Originally the athletes probably raced in full armour, but soon their panoply was reduced to helmet, shield (Fig. 6) and for a time greaves (Plate IIIb). It is hard to escape the impression that this event provided a slightly comic coda for an audience exhausted by a long day of racing, boxing, wrestling and the pankration. On the

* Only three or four of these coins survive, all in such poor condition that it proved impossible to obtain a suitable photograph for this book.

Fig. 6 Practising the race in armour (from an Athenian cup
of the late sixth century B.C.).

other hand, it remained in the programme from its introduction in
520 B.C. to the end.

Two other events made a brief appearance in the Games. The
boys' pentathlon was contested only once, in 628 B.C., and it was then
abandoned for reasons we do not know. The other was something of
an absurdity, a race of mule-carts (with seated drivers) drawn by pairs
of mules, introduced in 500 and dropped after the Games of 444 B.C.
Pausanias dismissed it as neither ancient nor dignified, and he was
right: an expensive sport, it lacked splendour; the mule was a pack-
animal, not an appropriate symbol of the equestrian aristocrat. Few
names of winners survive, though one of them, Anaxilas, tyrant of
Rhegium, was proud enough of 'his' victory to commemorate it on
his coins (Plate 23b). But he was a petty tyrant.

If we put aside these two temporary anomalies, the slow evolution
of the Olympic programme can be appreciated from the following
table, which shows the date when each event was first contested (all
B.C.) and the city or district from which the first victor came.

[42]

PLATE 1 (a) Spyridon Louis, a Greek, wins the marathon race at the first modern Olympic Games, in Athens in 1896, from a contemporary portrayal.

(b) At the end of a torch race the winner approaches the altar, heaped with kindling ready to be lit. The runners wear the diadems usual in the race and carry their torches in metal holders (see pp. 4-5). The bearded man alongside the altar is either a city official or a priest; the large jar may represent the prize common in this contest, and it would then have been filled with oil. From an Athenian red-figured 'bell krater', 36 cm high, dated about 430-420 B.C. The torch race was not part of the Olympic Games.

PLATE 2 (a) The marble tomb-stone of an aged lyric poet, possibly Pindar. (The word 'lyric' originated from the fact that odes were composed to be sung, usually by a chorus, to the accompaniment of a lyre.) On stylistic grounds, the tomb-stone, 94·5 cm × 65·5 cm, is dated to the second half of the fifth century B.C., and, since it was found in Boeotia, it is tempting to think that it commemorated Pindar, the greatest Boeotian poet, who died in 438 B.C. at the age of eighty.

(b) Part of a larger inscription which recorded the victories of a pan-kratiast whose name is lost. The surviving fragment lists victories at the Pythian and Nemean Games, and also at the Actian Games, which had been raised to Circuit rank to commemorate the victory of Augustus over Antony and Cleo-patra at Actium in 31 B.C. This stone dates from the second half of the first century B.C. and is embedded in a contemporary wall in Stratonicea in Asia Minor (photographed by H. W. Pleket in 1956).

PLATE 3 SACRIFICE

(a) Youths holding down a bull to be slaughtered for the sacrifice, while one of them, at the left, is sharpening the knife. The scene appears on the base of an Athenian red-figured cup shortly before 500 B.C.

(b) The sacrifice itself: an attendant is holding the meat from the thighs of the animal on a spit over the flames, while another attendant holds a sacrificial basket and the priest, at the far left, pours a libation over the fire. The presence of a crowned ithyphallic 'herm' (one of the most familiar religious objects in the Greek world, especially in Athens, to be found on boundaries, at city-gates, in front of houses and elsewhere as a device for warding off evil) suggests that Hermes is the god being honoured. This Athenian 'column krater' dates from about 420 B.C.

PLATES 4-5 Aerial view of Olympia today. The Stadium can be clearly seen at the right and the other buildings can be identified from the plans given in Figs. 7-10.

PLATE 6 GODS AND GODDESSES AT OLYMPIA

(a) The head of Zeus on a rare bronze coin of Elis, all three surviving copies having been found at Olympia (shown about twice actual size). The obverse has the head of the emperor Hadrian (A.D. 117-138), reproduced on Plate 30c. (For a much earlier portrait of Zeus on an Elean coin, see Plate 10a.)

(b) Zeus hurling a thunderbolt. A bronze statuette, 22·6 cm high, now in the Olympia Museum.

(c) Heracles holding the vault of heaven for Atlas—one of the sculptures on the frieze of the east front of the great temple of Zeus at Olympia.

(d) The head of Hera, probably from the great cult statue of the goddess which stood in the inner chamber (*cella*) of her temple, the first large one to be built at Olympia (Plate 8a). The style of the sculpture is Spartan, carved in limestone, 52 cm high.

PLATE 7 (a) Model of part of the main shrine at Olympia, showing, at the left, the Metroön, a small temple of the Mother of the Gods; top, the treasure-houses of a dozen Greek cities; below them, statues of Zeus paid for by fines. The model is by A. Mallwitz.

(b) A small bronze chariot and charioteer—a votive offering dedicated to Zeus at Olympia in the eighth century B.C., before the chariot race was introduced into the Games in 680. It is 8·7 cm high.

(c) Bronze tripod and cauldron, 61 cm high, probably of the ninth century B.C., found at Olympia. Such objects were frequently dedicated to gods at major shrines. Eventually they became the conventional symbol on painted vases for Games prizes (IIIb), presumably because of the references to tripods and cauldrons as 'treasure' in the Homeric poems.

PLATE 8 (a) Remains of the 'Doric' temple of Hera at Olympia, the oldest large building on the site, constructed of local limestone at the beginning of the sixth century B.C. The base measures 18·75 by 50·00 m, and the frame consists of 6 by 16 columns (counting each angle column twice).

(b) In order to provide a fuller impression of a Doric temple, this small picture shows the best preserved of all Greek temples, the marble Hephaesteum in Athens, built in the middle of the fifth century B.C. Its base measures 14·45 by 32·5 m, and the frame is 6 by 13 columns. The sculptures on this temple are devoted to the adventures of two heroes, Heracles and Theseus, and because of the latter the temple had been falsely identified in modern times and called the Theseum (see Plate 17b).

200 metres	776	Elis
400 metres	724	Elis
4800 metres	720	Sparta
Pentathlon	708	Sparta
Wrestling	708	Sparta
Boxing	688	Smyrna
Chariot race	680	Thebes
Horse race	648	Crannon (Thessaly)
Pankration	648	Syracuse
Boys' 200 metres	632	Elis
Boys' wrestling	632	Sparta
Boys' boxing	616	Sybaris
Race in armour	520	Heraea (Arcadia)

It will be immediately obvious that one can speak of the Olympic Games (in the plural) beginning in 776 B.C. only in retrospect. A single event, the 200-metre race, held before there was even a Stadium, hardly constitutes 'Games'. Yet the ancient tradition is so insistent about the 776 date that we cannot brush it aside; perhaps this was the first sacred contest in Greek history, as distinct from funeral games or mere pastimes. And many years were to pass before Olympia moved to Games in a proper sense. A second race was not added until the fourteenth Olympiad, the first non-racing event not until the eighteenth. Then the tempo of growth quickened slightly and the range was further extended; soon after the middle of the seventh century B.C. the classical shape of the Games was evident. The growing pan-Hellenism kept pace. Yet the astonishing conservatism of Olympia was not relaxed. After 520 B.C., only seven new competitions were introduced, and of these the two-horse chariot race and three equestrian contests for colts require no more than a passing notice.

We should, however, pause over the other three novelties. In 396 B.C. competitions began for heralds and trumpeters, the precise nature of which is unknown. Although both appear to breach the rule that the otherwise familiar musical and dramatic contests were excluded at Olympia, they were peculiar and explicable exceptions: heralds and trumpeters were essential functionaries in the Games, and after nearly four centuries they, too, were given the opportunity to win an olive wreath. Then, at long last, in 200 B.C. the boys' pankration, popular throughout the Greek world for hundreds of years, was given a place in the Olympic Games. That was the final innovation.

Why did the Olympic officials resist the boys' pankration for centuries? Not, certainly, because they thought the pankration too brutal for youngsters, who were permitted to box, after all. The fact is that we do not know, any more than we know why individual events were introduced when they were. There is a story that the winner of the first boxing event, Onomastos of Smyrna, also laid down the rules for the contest. If true, this tale suggests that boxing was not then very widespread in the Peloponnese, so that the Olympic rules had to be borrowed from Asia Minor, where the sport was better developed. It must be emphasized that no Olympic event was first invented there. They were all familiar throughout Hellas, and the sole question was whether or not a particular contest would be raised to Olympic status.

Another story, which deserves credence, explains one (perhaps temporary) change in the order of events, of which there were presumably not a few in the history of the Games. In 212 B.C. the two favourites in the pankration were a local athlete named Caprus and Clitomachus of Thebes. The latter was also entered in boxing, the former in wrestling, which he proceeded to win. Clitomachus then appealed to the judges to bring the pankration forward on the ground that he risked serious injury in boxing—a nice confirmation of the ancient view that boxing was more dangerous than either wrestling or the pankration. The judges agreed, though that decision was against the interest of their own man from Elis. And they were rewarded for their virtue: Clitomachus lost to Caprus in the pankration finals, and then won in the boxing.

Such fairness, rising above local patriotism, was not always evident. By and large, however, the Olympic Games were free from partisan excesses, from the pull of fashion, from the pressures of wealth and class. After the middle of the fifth century B.C., lower-class athletes began to participate in increasing numbers. Some gentlemen, like the Athenian Alcibiades, openly expressed their dislike of this encroachment upon their noble prerogatives. The considerable cost protected their privileged status in the equestrian games, and these were the men who welcomed, and possibly stimulated, the introduction of additional equestrian events after 408 B.C. But for every Alcibiades there were for a long time enough men of his social position who were willing and even eager not only to race in the Games but also to have a go at the tough sports. Aratus of Sicyon, who was to become the leading Greek statesman of his generation, won the Olympic chariot race (as owner) in 232 B.C., but he was also the victor in several pentathlons, though perhaps never in the Olympics. By coincidence, the Olympic pentathlon winner in that same year, 232 B.C., another Peloponnesian, Gorgos of Messenia, 'second to none of the Messenians in wealth and birth' and 'the most renowned of all those who sought wreaths in the Games', went on to become equally renowned in politics.

One final example of Olympic conservatism is noteworthy. Women had traditionally been restricted to contests of their own during special festivals held at times other than the period of the great Games. At Olympia, for example, there was one in honour of Zeus' consort Hera, which included a sprint for girls over a distance of about 160 metres. However, towards the end of the pre-Christian era, increasing emancipation of women, especially in the cities, led to the introduction of short-distance races for girls in many of the Games, including the three other Games of the Circuit. Olympia resisted, as usual, just as it held out against the admission of women as spectators. There is a splendid cautionary tale about this. In 404 B.C. a widow, who came from a great sporting family of wealthy Rhodian exiles, wished to watch her son box in the boys' event at the Olympic Games. She went disguised as a trainer, but, in her excitement when the boy won, she leaped over the barrier behind which the trainers were stationed and exposed herself. The judges let her off without penalty 'out of respect for her father and her brothers and her son, all of whom were Olympic winners', but a rule was immediately introduced requiring trainers henceforth to attend the contests as naked as the participants.

Institutional hardening of the arteries is a familiar phenomenon in sports as in other activities throughout history. But the usual price is decline and eventual death. The Olympic Games, on the contrary, gained renewed strength from their conservatism and their stability. They stood at the apex from the beginning of the Circuit, and there they remained for a thousand years, impervious to popular fashion, to complicated political and cultural changes, to imperial whim, to the challenge of every competing attraction, old or new.

4

Spectators and Facilities

For the first modern Olympic Games, in Athens in 1896, a spacious new stadium was built (Plate 1a). And since then a new stadium has been constructed, usually grander than its predecessor, or an older one refurbished, for each of the succeeding Games. We take this practice so much for granted that we run the danger of reading our ideas back into antiquity, and of getting the flavour of the ancient Games wrong as a result.

For some two hundred years after 776 B.C., while a large part of the classical programme was slowly introduced, Olympia offered no physical facilities to speak of, neither for spectators nor for the athletes. One might almost say that there was no architecture, only a sacred precinct of Zeus in a pastoral setting.* Apart from the little shrine of the legendary Pelops and a scattering of altars, there were no stone buildings, no temples, no large statuary, not even a distinct space set aside for the races. All the events were conducted within the open precinct, near the altar of Zeus, save for the equestrian events

* The physical history of Olympia which follows, based chiefly on modern archaeological excavation, is presented diagrammatically in Figs. 7-10 and photographically from the air (Plates 4-5).

Plans of Olympia showing the architectural history of the site. Not every building has been identified on these plans (and the purpose of some is still unknown).

Fig. 7 Sixth and fifth centuries B.C. The asterisks indicate those buildings constructed after 500 B.C.

Fig. 8 Fourth century B.C.

Fig. 9 Hellenistic age—third to first centuries B.C.

Fig. 10 Roman empire—first to third centuries A.D.

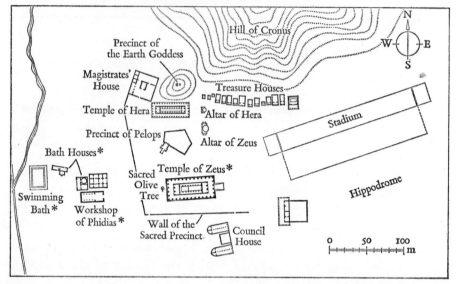

Fig. 7

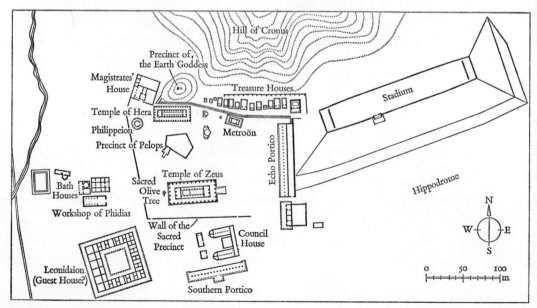

Fig. 8

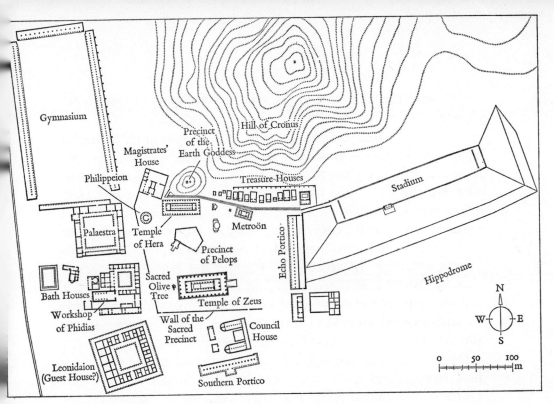

Fig. 9

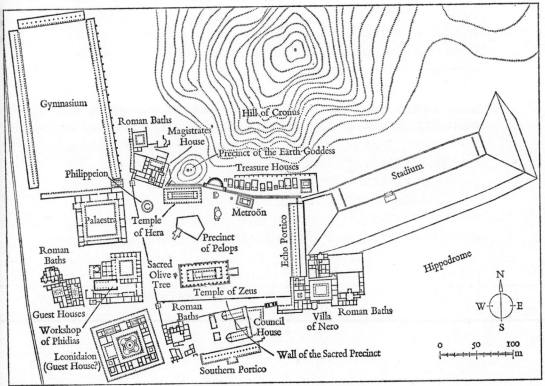

Fig. 10

which were probably held in the area later occupied by the Hippodrome.

Then, in the sixth century B.C., a great development set in, lasting about two centuries, accompanying the emergence of the Olympic Games as the apex of the pan-Hellenic Circuit. Among the first of the new buildings were the large stone temple of Zeus' consort Hera (Plate 8a); the twelve treasure-houses on a ridge above (Plate 7a), the construction of which demonstrates the new importance of Olympia and the volume of sacred treasure that was accumulating; the Council-House, reflecting the existence of a larger and busier management than had been needed heretofore. And the first Stadium was laid out slightly to the east of the precinct but still not separated from it, with an artificial earth embankment for spectators. The Stadium was improved about the middle of the fifth century, and in the fourth century B.C. it was moved less than one hundred metres east to its final location and given the dimensions and layout that are still visible on the ground (Plate 18a). Additional embankments for spectators were built up on the eastern and western sides; the judges' stand was erected (Fig. 4) and a wall and colonnade were constructed separating the Stadium from the sacred precinct, not because the Games had lost any of their religious status but because the vastly increased crowds required it.

This substantial building programme required money. Admission to all Games was free throughout their history, and though the wealthier aristocrats of Elis were not mean, with either their own or public funds, their purses were not unlimited. So, as was common throughout Greek and Roman history, other communities and wealthy individuals were also called upon from time to time. In a sense, there was a permanent open invitation for contributions, and sometimes crude hints were thrown out, as when the Eleans themselves erected statues of Hellenistic rulers. What Elis lacked, in their unwarlike condition, was the opportunity to use captured wealth for the ornamentation of Olympia. Once, however, when they conquered the district of Pisatis about 470 B.C., they used their booty to begin the erection of an appropriate temple, at last, to their patron deity, Zeus. Built of local limestone by a local architect named Libon, the new temple stood on a foundation which measured 27·7 by 64·1 m, almost twice the area of the earlier temple of Hera. In the next generation the Eleans engaged Phidias, the most famous and most reputed sculptor of the century, to make a great statue of the god, seated on his throne and decked out in gold and ivory; it was housed in the inner chamber of the now completed temple, where it towered to the roof (Fig. 11).* It soon ranked as one of the Seven Wonders of the World.

What facilities were provided for the athletes, one becomes impatient to discover, and the surprising answer is—hardly anything apart from the Stadium and the Hippodrome. The gymnasium and palaestra date from the third or second century B.C. Until then the competitors were compelled to train and practise in the open air. One or two bath-houses were built rather early on, but the first, rather sparse hostel not before the fourth century B.C., and that had to be shared by athletes, their trainers, officials and important visitors. A second guest-house and more baths were eventually added, and that is all—not even a pale shadow of a modern Olympic village. To be sure, wealthy Hellenistic monarchs and Roman dignitaries, like Agrippa, son-in-law of Augustus, the first Roman emperor, made benefactions, but more often for impressive monuments that would memorialize themselves rather than for the functional needs of the Games. Thus, the curious round building known as the Philippeion was erected under Philip and Alexander in order to house statues of all the members of the royal Macedonian dynasty. In the following century, statues of King Ptolemy II of Egypt and his sister-wife, Queen Arsinoe, were set up by the Egyptian admiral Callicrates (on a base 24 metres long).

There was one outstanding utilitarian exception: in the second

---

* Among the more recent archaeological discoveries at Olympia are the remains of Phidias' vast workshop, and, in the debris, a pottery cup with his name scratched on it (Plate 10c). It was the surviving shell of the workshop that the Christian community at Olympia converted into a church in about A.D. 400.

Fig. 11 This statue of Zeus in gold and ivory was one of 'The Seven
Wonders of the World' and was made by Phidias in the second half
of the fifth century B.C. Placed in the inner chamber (*cella*) of the
great temple of Zeus, it was more than 12 m high, and the smaller
figure of the goddess Victory (Nike) was about 2 m. Ancient critics
complained about the proportions: if the god stood up, they noted, he
would go through the roof. (See also Plate 10a.) This reconstruction
by F. Adler was made from representations of the statue on coins
from the ruins of the temple.

century A.D. an Athenian named Herodes Atticus (Plate 30d), probably the richest Greek of his time, built an elaborate water-supply
and sanitation system. By carefully constructed channels, the water
was brought from a distance of more than one kilometre to a large
semi-circular colonnade, twelve or thirteen metres high, surmounted
by statues of Herodes himself, his family and his favourite Roman
emperors (Fig. 12). Then, from this 'shrine of the Nymphs' towering
over the precinct, the water was fed to a network of fountains and

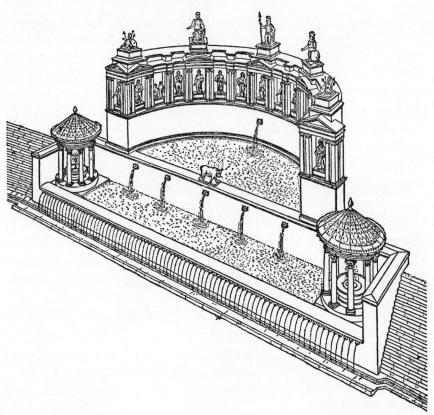

Fig. 12 'The shrine of the Nymphs', the dominant element in the elaborate water-supply system provided for Olympia by Herodes Atticus soon after the middle of the second century A.D. It stood between the temple of Hera and the Treasure Houses. The re-construction is by Hans Schleif.

channels below. The second-century date is worth stressing: for nearly a thousand years Olympia had got along with inadequate water—supplied by springs, cisterns and the river, which fortunately did not dry up in the summer—and with the most rudimentary sanitation.

Spectators had an even harder time of it. They watched the games from the embankments, sitting or standing on the ground; the few seats, some of marble (Plate 24b), were reserved for a handful of notables. Some primitive inns may have been available in the immediate neighbourhood, but they could not have been numerous or attractive. Who would invest in such an enterprise in an undeveloped area for one week's business every four years? The overwhelming majority of visitors slept in the open air or in tents and relied on itinerant food and drink purveyors (as they depended on migrant entertainers to amuse them when the day's events had ended). Heat, noise and dust are frequently mentioned by ancient writers to characterize the Olympic week. 'They say', writes Pausanias, 'that when Heracles was sacrificing at Olympia he was badly pestered by flies, so he invented or was taught by someone the sacrifice to Zeus Apomyios (Averter of Flies). The Eleans are said to sacrifice to Zeus Apomyios in the same way, to drive away flies from Olympia.' Not even Zeus, however, was likely to have that much power against the lack of sanitary facilities.

A disobedient slave, it is said, was once threatened by his owner with a visit to Olympia as a punishment. Apocryphal no doubt, but not meaningless, as the first-century A.D. Stoic writer and teacher Epictetus testifies in one of his *Discourses*, all the better a witness for the fact that, an ex-slave, he was known for his modest, not to say frugal, way of life.

> But some unpleasant and hard things happen in life. —And do they not happen at Olympia? Do you not swelter? Are you not cramped and crowded? Do you not bathe badly? Are you not drenched whenever it rains? Do you not have your fill of tumult and shouting and other annoyances? But I fancy that you bear and endure it all by balancing it off against the memorable character of the spectacle.

Policing tens of thousands of excited Greeks crowded into a relatively small area could not have been easy. An official corps of whip-bearers was on hand, who kept order among both spectators and athletes. Policing the innumerable pedlars was also essential. Normally a Greek city appointed a temporary market-commissioner for such special occasions, with the power to impose fines on the spot. It is unimaginable that Olympia did otherwise, despite the paucity of evidence. And it was characteristic of the Games that even this post was an honorific one, reserved for such Elean aristocrats as L. Vetulanus Laetus, market-commissioner for the Olympic year of A.D. 85, whose daughter or grand-daughter was the last recorded lady 'winner' of an Olympic chariot-race.

And yet the people came in the tens of thousands to the greatest recurring attraction of the Greek world. There was probably no other regular occasion in the ancient world when so many people were on the road (or the sea) for the same destination at the same time. In the early days, when there were only one, then two, then three races, held on a single day, the numbers of both athletes and spectators were small, drawn from a restricted area of the Peloponnese. One judge, who was also president of the games, sufficed. But as new events were added and competitors came from the western Greeks and from Asia Minor, and as a single day's festival grew into the five-day Games, spectators came to be counted in the thousands and then in the tens of thousands. Since there was no stadium with seats, it is impossible to get a precise estimate of numbers. However, one modern calculation, that forty thousand people could crowd into the Stadium, is plausible. The number of judges kept pace: it was increased to two in about 570, to nine early in the fifth century B.C. and almost immediately to ten.

Not everyone who came was a sports fan. Cicero, very much an intellectual, disapproved of those of his upper-class Roman compatriots, in the late first century B.C., who considered a visit to Olympia to be a necessary part of the grand tour, with Phidias' statue of Zeus as the central attraction. It cannot be doubted, however, that the games were what drew the great majority or that over the centuries there were shifts in the relative popularity of the different events. The fact that the largest number of Pindar's odes celebrated victors in the chariot race, the next largest being for pankration winners, reflects the value-system of the richest of the competitors, not necessarily that of the poorer athletes or of the spectators. The pentathlon also produced a divergence in the valuation. It seems not to have been much favoured by the crowds, and poorer athletes, with their pressing need to make their skills pay, would have found the necessary training for five different events too much of a burden. Many of their wealthy rivals, on the other hand, retained an attraction for the old aristocratic virtue of versatility, of the all-rounder, as did the moralists who disliked all forms of over-specialization.

Without attendance figures it is impossible to assess the relative popularity of the different events accurately, and we can therefore never be certain about this point in the Circuit. However, on the reasonable assumption that popularity was more or less the same in all Games, there is a good clue in those which offered money or other valuable prizes. In the boys' events at the Panathenaic Games in the fourth century B.C., the highest prize, 50 large jars (known as *amphoras*) filled with olive oil, went to the winner of the 200-metre dash. The pankration ranked second, with 40 jars, followed at the bottom by wrestling and the pentathlon, 30 each. These figures may still reflect the power of tradition rather than crowd pull: the sprint was the oldest and most venerable of all events. Yet even at that relatively early date, the pankration had already moved into second place.

Another set of figures, these from local games in Aphrodisias in Asia Minor in the second century A.D., is perhaps more realistic. They are as follows (in cash prizes): pankration, 3000 drachmas; 200-metre race, 1250; 400 metres, 1000; long-distance race, 750; pentathlon, a paltry 500.* Popularity is the explanation of the enormous variation;

* For these sums of money, see the preliminary note at the beginning of the book. Our information unfortunately does not permit us to express the value of the Panathenaic oil-prizes in monetary terms, especially since the recipients were free to sell both the oil and the jars, which were much esteemed in such distant places as central Italy (by the Etruscans), Cyrene and southern Russia. Of the six illustrated in this volume, two (Plates IV, VIIb) were found in the district of Cyrene, the other four (Plates Va, VIIa, IIb, 21) in Etruscan tombs.

the athletes were all equally professional, drawn from the same classes of society, and they had no other basis for claiming larger prizes in one event against another.

Presumably a higher proportion of Olympic spectators came from Elis and neighbouring regions, given the expense and difficulties of long journeys in antiquity. That would have affected their loyalties (and we shall see that the fact that the judges were always Elean led to occasional accusations of unfairness). Crowds at ancient Games were as partisan, as volatile and as excitable as at any other period of time. 'None of the horses will run more slowly if you behave with decorum', said the famous orator Dio of Prusa, known as Dio Chrysostom ('Golden-tongued'), in a public oration in Alexandria soon after A.D. 100. 'Who can describe your shouts, the commotion and the agony, the bodily contortions and groans, the awful curses you utter? If you were not merely watching horses race—and horses that are used to racing—but were driven by the whips of tragedy, you would not be affected so cruelly.'

A revealing story is told about the Olympic Games of 212 B.C., when the champion boxer Clitomachus of Thebes (who, we remember, had the pankration brought forward on a plea of fairness) was matched against one Aristonicus, a protégé of King Ptolemy IV of Egypt. The large audience, according to the report of a good, near-contemporary historian,

immediately cheered him on, because they were pleased that someone had the courage to stand up to Clitomachus. As the bout continued, Aristonicus showed himself equal to it. When he landed a well-placed punch, there was a burst of applause and shouts of 'Keep up your courage, Aristonicus'. Clitomachus then stepped back, caught his breath, turned to the audience and asked them why they were cheering Aristonicus and supporting him as hard as they could. 'Have I committed a foul or broken the rules? Do you not know that I am fighting for the glory of Greece, Aristonicus for that of King Ptolemy? Would you prefer an Egyptian to carry off the Olympic wreath by beating Greeks, or a Theban and a Boeotian to be the world's boxing champion?' When the spectators heard these words of Clitomachus, it is reported, they suffered such a change of heart that Aristonicus was eventually beaten, more by the temper of the crowd than by Clitomachus.

The underdog was clearly as much the favourite with Olympic crowds as everywhere. National loyalties did not prevail spontaneously or 'naturally', but they could be worked up. And then, an audience drawn heavily from Elis and nearby regions identified themselves with a Theban boxer, Greeks against the 'barbarian'. The conquests of Alexander the Great and the ensuing Hellenization of Egypt, Syria and other parts of the Near East brought more and more competitors to the Games whose 'Greekness' was rather dubious. Some prejudice resulted, not surprisingly. Yet—and this is far more important—the boxer Aristonicus was only one of a long series of athletes from Egypt, and there is no trace in our records of actual discrimination against them by the judges or the spectators. Earlier, and perhaps more surprisingly, Anaxilas, tyrant of Rhegium in southern Italy, carried off the prize in the mule-cart race in the same year, 480 B.C., in which he allied himself with the Carthaginians in their invasion of Greek Sicily, thrown back at the battle of Himera.

Nor was there any social discrimination, as more and more competitors of lower-class origin appeared. For all Pindar's snobbishness or Alcibiades' refusal to enter after 416 B.C. on the ground that the Games had been contaminated by riff-raff, neither official policy nor public opinion was in the least influenced. It was a common debating-trick in Greek politics to sneer at an opponent's disreputable antecedents. But hardly ever in a Games context. Every competitor had the same formal rights, under the same rules, and could claim the same prize if he won; only his own skill and strength mattered. In a world of built-in inequalities, that was a significant rarity.

PLATE 9 (a) Achilles organized funeral games in honour of his friend Patroclus. The lower band shows the chariot race (see also Plate IIb) with the names of the charioteers: Odysseus (not shown), Hippothoon, Damasippus, Diomedes and Antimedon (not shown). Except for Diomedes, the names are all different from those in the *Iliad* account. The painter clearly knew the tradition about these games but apparently not the details of the Homeric version. The upper band shows a boar hunt. The two javelin-throwers in the middle have the same type of finger-thong used with the javelin in the Olympic Games.

These two bands are from the so-called François Vase, one of the largest and most elaborate specimens of Athenian painted pottery, a two-handled basin, painted by Clitias about 575 B.C., 66 cm tall, found in the cemetery of the Etruscan city of Chiusi, now in the Archaeological Museum in Florence.

(b) A runner on the starting-line, probably a votive offering, with the words 'I belong to Zeus' inscribed down the right thigh. A bronze statuette of the early fifth century B.C., 10·2 cm high, found at Olympia.

PLATE 10 (a) The head of Zeus wearing a wreath of wild olive, which was the victor's award at the Olympic Games. Portrayed on a silver coin from Elis of about 420-410 B.C., the head is almost certainly copied from Phidias' great cult-statue of the god (see Fig. 11) completed only a few years earlier (about 2½ times actual size). (For the head of Zeus on an Elean bronze coin more than five hundred years later, see Plate 6a.)

(b) A crown of wild celery leaves, the victor's award at the Nemean Games, encircles the word NEMEIA. A bronze coin from Argos of the Roman imperial period (about 2½ times actual size).

The victor's wreath at the Pythian Games at Delphi was of laurel, and of pine branches at the Isthmian Games.

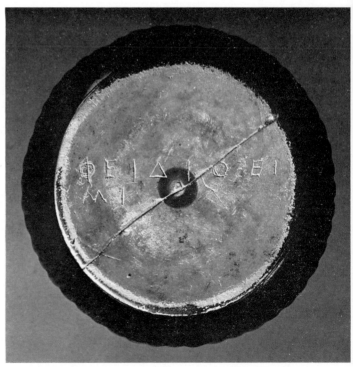

(c) Phidias had his own workshop at Olympia (see Fig. 7), and during the excavation of the ruins a pottery cup was found. Its base is rather crudely inscribed 'I belong to Phidias'.

PLATE 11 (a) The harnessing of a two-horse chariot. The picture clearly shows the form of the harness with the band round the lower throat of each horse. An Athenian black-figured vase of the sixth century B.C.

(b) The horse race. The horses were ridden bareback, since the saddle, an eastern invention, did not reach Europe before the Middle Ages (and the stirrup not before the first century A.D.).

This early Panathenaic amphora was awarded to the winner of the horse race (see p. 56 and the note to Plate Va). It was made about 500 B.C. or shortly before, and was found in an Etruscan tomb at Vulci.

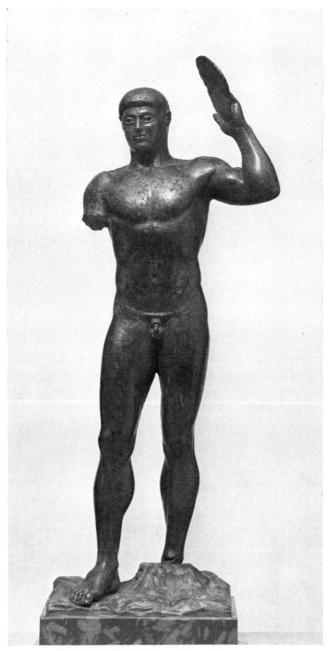

PLATE 12 A discus-thrower at the start of his throw.
He holds the discus in his left hand, before transferring
it to his right hand for the backward swing (as shown in
Plate 13). A bronze statuette made in Athens early in
the fifth century B.C., 23·5 cm tall.

PLATE 13 'The Discus-Thrower' or Discobolus by the Athenian sculptor Myron, about 450 B.C. It shows the discus-thrower having completed the backward swing of his arm, poised ready for the forward swing to the launch. It is thought that the discus was thrown in much the same way as today, though not with the circling movement within the marked ring.

This is probably the most famous, most admired and most frequently copied athletic statue ever made. The original, of hollow bronze, has long since disappeared, but copies in marble and bronze, life size or as statuettes, even on gems, were common throughout antiquity. The one shown here, in marble, is now in the Museum of the Diocletian Baths in Rome.

PLATE 14 A javelin-thrower, supervised by a trainer with a whip in his hand. The finger-thong is clearly shown (see Fig. 3 and Plate 9a). The style of throwing the javelin appears to have been almost the same as that used today apart from the use of the thong. An Athenian red-figured vase of the fifth century B.C.

PLATE 15 (a) A jumper in mid-air with jumping weights in his hands. The weights have been shown by modern experiments to increase the distance in a standing jump considerably. The youth at the left is using the weights much like modern dumb-bells, for exercises that appear to have nothing in particular to do with jumping. The scene is from an Athenian cup of about 500 B.C.

(b) A stone jumping weight with an inscription saying that it was dedicated by the Spartan, Akmatidas, to celebrate his victory in the pentathlon 'without a contest' (see p. 64). This weight was found at Olympia, to be dated about 500 B.C. These weights varied from 1·07 kg to 4·63 kg.

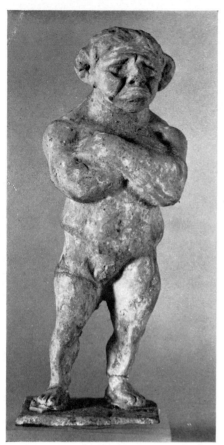

PLATE 16 The Greeks did not always take their athletes seriously and occasionally caricatured them (see also Fig. 13).

(a) Caricature of a muscular wrestler or pankratiast. Hellenistic terracotta statuette, 10 cm high.

(b) Dwarf boxer. Bronze statuette, 12·4 cm high, probably first or second century A.D., restored below the knees.

5

Rules and Officials

Since the Olympic Games were a religious festival, they were organized and managed by the state directly. That was the invariable rule throughout Greek history. And, as the state of Elis was always controlled by an oligarchy of rich gentleman-farmers (regardless of changes in the formal structure of government), so were the Games. Originally the king was in charge, but monarchy was replaced by oligarchy at an early, but unknown, date; thereafter, in each Olympiad, special officials with the pretentious title, 'Hellenic judges', were selected from among the nobility for that purpose. Their number, as we have already seen, was first increased to two, and early in the fifth century B.C. to ten, one from each of the districts into which Elis was subdivided. After a pre-selection procedure, possibly by popular vote on a narrow eligible list, the final choice was made by drawing lots, also a universal Greek procedure.

In office, their powers were extensive and almost absolute; appeal from their decisions was possible only to another official body, the Olympic Council created not later than about 400 B.C. We call them 'judges' but in reality they combined the roles of the modern Olympic committee, judges and umpires. While on duty, they wore special purple robes, the symbol of high status and even royalty, in this instance of the high honour they had attained by becoming Olympic judges. Honour implied and regularly entailed expense. Although we lack detail, the widespread practice among Greek cities suggests that the judges, who were unpaid, were expected to bear some share of the costs of the Games along with other members of the local nobility, in addition to the contribution from the public treasury. Although there was no prize-money and few training or residential facilities, and though the costs of building temples, altars and porticoes were not the responsibility of the Games officials, a substantial outlay was nevertheless required—for groundsmen, whip-bearers and other staff, slave or free; for the vast quantities of oil consumed by the athletes in their frequent massages; for maintenance; for all the incidentals of sacred processions, sacrifices and other ceremonies. The spectators, we remember, made no contribution directly through admission fees, though no doubt enough of the money they spent on their personal needs found its way into the pockets of the Elean gentlemen, who raised cattle and hemp for rope-making as local specialities in addition to the usual grain, wine and oil.

Neither the fundamental structure of the Games nor the rules for the individual events were within the prerogative of the judges, nor were basic changes. The decision to introduce the chariot race in 680 B.C., for example, or to add the boys' pentathlon in 628 and to drop it immediately thereafter, was too grave to be left to officials chosen by lot for a single set of Games. The latter were empowered to make minor adjustments, as they did in 212 B.C. when they moved the pankration ahead of the boxing competition, but nothing more fundamental. The rule-book was the work of a special commission, called 'law-codifiers' (*nomographoi*), acting under the authority of the government of Elis. They then briefed the judges at each Olympiad, whose duty it was to administer and interpret the rules.

That duty was, in fact, very broad, including not only the umpiring of the events but also a surprising (to us) range of powers in political, moral and psychological matters. The actual umpiring is the least interesting of all: the difficulties in deciding on a wrestling fall or a foul in the long jump are not essentially different from what they are today. Nor is the irreducible subjective element. Split decisions are on record (the judges divided into sub-committees as umpires); so are accusations of wrong decisions and of corruption and partisanship. They are neither illuminating nor unfamiliar.

Full-time work for the judges began one month before the Games began, the date at which all the competitors were required to be in Elis. Latecomers could appeal, if they had a valid excuse, such as illness, piracy or shipwreck, and that was the first decision that fell to the judges. Pausanias has a revealing story about the boxing event in the 218th Olympiad (A.D. 93). An Alexandrian boxer, Apollonius, nicknamed 'the Sprinkler', arrived late and gave as his excuse the contrary winds in the Aegean Sea. However, a fellow-Alexandrian, Heraclides, exposed the lie: the true explanation was that Apollonius had been busy picking up cash prizes in Games in Asia Minor and therefore sailed for Olympia too late. The judges disqualified him and awarded Heraclides the wreath without a contest. Apollonius lost his head—the 'market-value' of an Olympic victory was not lightly to be given up; he bound his hands with the thongs, rushed at Heraclides and punched him. For that he was penalized with a heavy fine, 'the first Egyptian convicted by the Eleans not for giving or taking a bribe but for dishonouring the Games' by his behaviour at the prize-giving.

The training month was also a busy period of establishing qualifications. There were no 'teams' or official entrants, despite the considerable interest individual Greek cities took in their own citizen-athletes. Each would-be competitor applied on his own; Alcibiades could even choose to enter seven chariots at one time. It was then up to the judges to accept or refuse. The first rule was that a competitor must be the legitimate son of free Greek parents (there was no 'grandfather clause'), without a criminal record, and officially registered on the citizen roster of his native city. Checking and enforcement of this rule would have been difficult enough, given the rudimentary state of public record-keeping in those days, but further complications were created by the Greek expansion into non-Greek territories, especially after the conquests of Alexander the Great, and by the need to show common sense in dealing with rulers and other powerful men outside the Greek world narrowly conceived.

Thus, in the fifth century B.C. an earlier King Alexander of Macedon produced a genealogy tracing his royal line back to Heracles. That satisfied the judges. So did a high official from Phoenician Sidon in the third century B.C., who recalled the mythological link between Sidon and Thebes. His good Greek name, Diotimus, no doubt helped (as would good spoken Greek), but it was not absolutely necessary. The plain fact is that neither the judges nor anyone else, including the spectators, showed any reluctance to shut their eyes to the requirement of Greekness (unlike the rule excluding slaves) when prudent opportunism suggested it. In all the many Olympic stories there is none about a serious dispute over this rule. And we may unhesitatingly assume that when the future Roman emperor Tiberius (not to mention Nero) entered a chariot in the race, perhaps in 4 B.C., he did not even have to go through the motions of providing a fictitious family-tree.

More troublesome, apparently, were the decisions created by the introduction of boys' events. The judges could not possibly have controlled age-claims of applicants coming from all corners of the Greek world. They trusted to their eyes and their common sense, instead, with the aim of preventing blatant mismatches. Those near the minimum age of twelve were admitted or not, as the case may have been, according to a subjective judgment of their possibilities, especially in the body-contact sports. As they approached the eighteen-year upper end, they might, from similar considerations, be classified as men regardless of their own assertions. We are told, for example, of a fourth-century B.C. Spartan named Eualces, whose height and strength threatened to disqualify him from the boys' events, and who therefore took the precaution of having King Agesilaus of Sparta put pressure on the judges. He was then accepted as a 'boy', but he failed to score a victory. Another story, about 'the first man to box scientifically', Pythagoras of Samos (not to be confused with the philosopher of the same name), relates that he entered the Olympic boys' competition in 588 B.C., was excluded by the judges, and promptly transferred to the men's event which he won.

Concern for the quality of the competition explains one additional, and rather mysterious, ground for disqualification (or for a fine), and that was to enter an event 'merely in order to spite an opponent'. A more difficult rule to interpret, requiring a decision about a man's state of mind, is hard to imagine. In 480 B.C., Theogenes, a distinguished citizen of Thasos, entered for both the boxing and the pankration. He wore himself out in winning the former against Euthymus of Locri, victor in the previous Olympiad, and consequently withdrew from the pankration. Thereupon the judges levied the huge fine of 12,000 drachmas on him, one half to be paid to Zeus, the other to Euthymus personally, because, they said, he had entered two events solely with the intention to spite the champion boxer. Theogenes naturally refused to pay the private fine, but four years later he paid his 6000-drachma debt to Zeus, entered the pankration contest and won it, leaving a clear field for Euthymus to carry off the boxing prize for a second time (and a third time in 472).

What we are to make of this seemingly implausible story is anyone's guess. Theogenes was (along with Milo of Croton) the most famous athlete in Greek history, about whom a clutch of improbable tales and outright legends gradually arose. He was the son of Heracles, and much else, as we shall see later. Yet there may be a kernel of truth in the story of the enormous fine of 480 B.C.; that the pankration was too much even for such a genius immediately after a gruelling boxing-match is shown by the successful appeal by Clitomachus, at a later date, to have the order of the two events reversed.

Those who survived the preliminary investigations spent a full month in training under strict supervision, having sworn by Zeus Horkios that they had already been training during the whole of the previous ten months. The judges laid down a regimen of exercises, often improvised. They were free to disregard the wishes or training habits of the individual athletes; protest was unavailing and the ultimate sanction was exclusion from the Games. The judges also organized trial matches, another strange proceeding by our standards. The purpose was not related to the draw, which was also the judges' responsibility, for seeding was unknown. But one consequence, whether intended or not, was that the experience in the trial matches not infrequently led to withdrawals before the Games got under way, especially in wrestling, boxing and the pankration, contests in which chance and accident were at a minimum. That helps explain the surviving boasts of victory without opposition. As the number of Games increased measurably, furthermore, the number of Olympic entries in these three sports seems eventually to have declined. The other Games thus served the same purpose as the trial matches in Olympia. When one or two stars were known to have entered, lesser fry abandoned the contest in advance. There could be no greater tribute to the supremacy of the Olympic Games in the eyes of the athletes themselves.

In many Games it was permissible to withdraw while the Games were already under way, even after several rounds in a particular event. One wrestler boasted that in Games in Asia Minor his opponents withdrew as soon as they saw him undressed. About A.D. 200 the Olympic pankratiast M. Aurelius Asclepiades included in a long list of the special features that illuminated his career the fact that some contestants withdrew from the beginning, others in the first or second round of the draw. A Rhodian long-distance runner, twice victor in the Olympic Games, once won the Isthmian prize 'because none of his opponents wished to compete'. And a very successful pentathlist, who won in three of the Circuit Games but failed at Olympia, proudly announced that in the Panhellenic Games in Athens he alone had participated in the formal entry procession, which means that all the others had scratched after discovering his presence in the assemblage prepared to contest in the Stadium.

At Olympia, however, all such moves were forbidden the moment the practice period was past. One unfortunate athlete, a pankratiast named Sarapion, who in about A.D. 25 fled just before the contest was to begin, was fined for his cowardice, the only occasion in Olympic history, according to Pausanias, when the judges were impelled to penalize on that charge. Since there was no second or third prize, rational recognition of superior power was acceptable, but postponing the exercise of reason until after the formal opening of the Games was cowardice.

Once the Games were actually under way, the judges had to contend with yet another question, apart from their duties as umpires, and that was bribery. It would have been miraculous if an issue which has bedevilled sport ever since competitive events were first introduced had not arisen at the Olympic Games. It would also be a near-miracle if we could assess Olympic corruption with any confidence at this distance in time. Attested instances are relatively few in our surviving evidence. The earliest case, Pausanias was told, occurred in 388 B.C. when Eupolus of Thessaly bribed three other boxers, one the winner at the previous Games, to allow him to gain the prize. In the next case, half a century later, an Athenian pentathlist won by similar corruption. The city of Athens sent its leading orator and politician, Hypereides, to Elis to plead for suspension of the fine. He failed and the city itself paid the money, but only after Apollo at Delphi threatened not to provide any more oracles for Athens until this was done. In 68 B.C., Rhodes came to the rescue of a wrestler in the same way, apparently without divine compulsion.

It is only in the Roman Empire that we hear, in general statements, of widespread corruption.* A third-century A.D. writer, Philostratus, not at all unfriendly to athletes and Games, complains that athletes accustomed to a luxurious way of life preferred throwing matches for money to the toil required for victory and prize-money; that vicious trainers encouraged them by lending them money at usurious rates of interest and then arranging the bribes in order to insure repayment. He adds, significantly, that the Olympic Games were free from such

* Before we rush to conclude that systematic corruption was therefore a late development in the history of ancient Games, we should remember that the earlier treatises on athletics have not survived.

malpractices. Curiously, none of this is ever linked with gambling. The Greeks were enthusiastic gamblers, chiefly with dice, and betting by spectators is already mentioned in the Homeric account of the funeral games for Patroclus. But there were no bookmakers, no professional syndicates, and bribery at Games was effectively limited to the athletes themselves or their families, the objective being to win a contest, not a large bet. Curiously, too, the practice—one might even say the rule—was that bribery proved after the event did not deprive the winner of his title and his wreath, heavily though he may have been punished otherwise.

Two of the penalties available to the judges have already been mentioned: fines and exclusion from the Games. The money from the fines was used to erect statues of Zeus (Plate 7a) inscribed with appropriate couplets: one, for example, erected on the first occasion, was designed (in Pausanias' paraphrase) 'to show that you win at Olympia with the speed of your feet and the strength of your body, not with money'. Exclusion was of course the ultimate sanction, if, for example, an offender refused or failed to pay his fine. The story of Theogenes suggests that the judges, with their characteristic eye on the larger issues, did not rush to impose the ultimate sanction, at least not when anyone as celebrated as Theogenes was involved. Nor have we any reason to believe that the managers of other Games blackballed anyone who had been barred from Olympic participation. But then, every ambitious athlete of that calibre would normally have gone to considerable lengths to avoid being denied his chance at the greatest prize of all. More than glory and honour was at stake: financially, too, he would have been much worse off.

A third form of punishment, flogging, deserves special notice because it is so surprising, especially in a Greek context. The Greeks were quite clear about this: flogging and other forms of corporal punishment (excluding the death penalty) were strictly reserved for slaves. The Roman approach was different, but not until Greece was incorporated in the Roman Empire was the old rigid Greek distinction in this matter eroded. It is therefore astounding that from very early times the Olympic judges were permitted to flog offending athletes, for violating training rules, for committing fouls or for bribery. One case became celebrated. In 420 B.C. Sparta was excluded from the Games because she was technically at war with Elis. A high Spartan official and diplomat, named Lichas, whose father had two Olympic chariot victories to his credit, craved the wreath so badly that he entered a chariot under a false registration, using a Boeotian name. His team won and he then challenged fate by going up to the judges to claim his prize, thereby exposing his fraud and getting himself scourged. Lichas was an enemy at the moment, to be sure, and one wonders whether the judges did not normally prefer to fine rather than flog an offender of high social or political status or of pan-Hellenic popularity. Yet the whip is so common in the illustrations we have (Plates 14, 22) that we must accept this oddity at face value.

Once, in 396 B.C., when the umpires split two to one in awarding the decision to an Elean sprinter over a rival from Ambracia, the Olympic Council overruled the majority and fined them to boot. That raises the final difficult question of the partisanship and honesty of the officials, at least when Elean athletes were involved. Who can say that the two umpires who were overruled in 396 B.C. had been consciously dishonest in deciding that their local sprinter was the winner in a photo-finish? There was naturally some sensitivity on the subject. Herodotus repeats a legendary tale that, in the early days, an Elean delegation went to consult the wise men of Egypt about the fairness of their Games rules, and were advised that justice was impossible unless the Eleans either turned the administration over to others or never themselves entered any event. But it is probably not fictitious that, following the victory of one of the judges in two equestrian events in 364 B.C., it was ruled that no judge could again compete.

We are reduced to the trite, rather boring conclusion that human frailty was not absent at Olympia, but that, on the other hand, it is unlikely that the Games could have retained their pre-eminence for a thousand years, under strictly local management, if flagrant abuse of that monopoly were repeated and common.

[67]

6

The Athletes

When the Alexandrian boxer Apollonius missed his chance at Olympia in A.D. 93 because he was too busy touring the Games in Asia Minor, the number of Games had grown from approximately fifty in 500 B.C. to over three hundred. The Olympic long-distance winner in A.D. 85, T. Flavius Metrobius of Iasos in Asia Minor, scored 140 wins altogether; an Asia Minor wrestler, who won at Olympia in 177, listed a total of 156 first prizes, divided between 29 in sacred Games and 127 in prize Games. The precision of the figures for non-sacred Games was a fairly new phenomenon—Pindar and writers of epigrams in the earlier period were satisfied with 'innumerable' or 'victories which it is not easy to enumerate'. And the number of athletes who travelled from one competition to another must have become much larger as the opportunities increased. Yet in the first half of the fifth century B.C. the great Theogenes of Thasos had already won twenty-two times in boxing and twice in the pankration in the Circuit alone (once in each at Olympia), besides apparently hundreds of victories in other Games, all in a twenty-two-year career.*

* An inscription in Delphi claimed 1300 other victories for him, including at least one as a long-distance runner, but that mathematically impossible, and suspiciously round, figure is a sign of his 'heroization' (to which we shall return in a later chapter), with its accompanying crop of legends.

A contemporary Athenian aristocrat named Callias recorded, on a marble statue-base on the Acropolis of his city, twelve Circuit victories in the pankration between 484 and 472 B.C., one of them in the Olympic Games.

Callias went on to play an important part in Athenian politics. As an adolescent and young adult, however, he must have devoted himself largely, if not entirely, to his favourite sport. So too did Theogenes, and Apollonius of Alexandria more than five hundred years later. The Greek world had come a long way from Homer's time, when Ajax and Odysseus and all the other nobles rode chariots, raced, boxed and threw the javelin as a pastime, as the leisure activity appropriate to warriors and chieftains of their social class. At least from the time when the Olympic programme became diversified and began to attract competitors from southern Italy, Sicily and Asia Minor, that is, not later than 700 or 680 B.C., games-playing (in the Greek sense) became increasingly a profession marked by specialization, and it remained that until the end of antiquity.

The narrow range of specialization comes out clearly from our surviving evidence about Olympic victors. One instance is the low status of the pentathlon, requiring such different skills as sprinting, throwing the discus and wrestling. The rarity of double victories in the two short-distance races is another proof. In 512 B.C. one man won the 200-metre sprint, the 400 metres and the race in armour on the same day, the first triple winner in Olympic racing history, and there were no more than half a dozen in over a thousand years. When Caprus of Elis defeated Clitomachus in the pankration in 212 B.C. immediately after having gained the wrestling prize, he was 'the first mortal since Heracles' to achieve that (and the first of only eight). The second was Aristomenes of Rhodes in 156 B.C. That was a great Olympic year for Rhodes: another of its citizens, named Leonidas, was a triple racing victor for the third time in succession, and he went on to repeat in 152 as well.*

* Our victor lists are incomplete, to be sure, but it is precisely the notable achievements that have survived, so that we are unlikely to have missed many

There is no reason to believe that the story was fundamentally different in the other Games. What was different about the Olympics (and the Circuit as a whole) was only their superior ability to attract the champions. Homer's nobles had disappeared from society, and both cities and individuals had to adjust their athletic procedures and values accordingly. The world of the Greek city-state may have been a long distance both in time and in character from the day, under Roman imperial rule, when an unidentified city in Asia Minor paid an Olympic winner 30,000 drachmas to enter the local Games (a Roman soldier was then paid between 225 and 300 drachmas a year). However, that extreme instance is merely the furthest possible extension of athletic professionalism and specialization that had set in not later than 700 B.C.

Any section of the Greek world that failed to adjust soon found itself left behind in the competition for Olympic glory. The notable example of Sparta deserves a moment of our time. After the early conquest and subjugation of neighbouring Messenia, the Spartan citizen-body, which was small (never numbering more than 10,000 adult males), was converted into a full-time, inflexible military machine. Rigorous physical training and a barracks life from the age of seven gave Spartans superiority in running, among other things; they produced about half the Olympic victors down to 600 B.C., predominantly in the racing events and the pentathlon. In the end, however, sergeant-majors could not compete with the professional trainers who emerged elsewhere in Greece by 600, nor could their pupils match the increasingly specialized athletes. Sparta stressed 'virtue', guts, strength, endurance, against 'art' (*techne*) and paid the price: the percentage of Spartan Olympic winners dropped to under forty in the sixth century B.C., to barely twenty in the following century, and the majority of those were in the equestrian events, where money counted, not skill. Characteristically, the Spartans found

---

multiple winners in the running events. The records are perhaps less complete for double winners in the body-contact sports.

a suitable explanation. Over-specialized athletes make poor soldiers, they said, and besides, since no real Spartan ever surrendered, they could not compete on equal terms in boxing and the pankration under Olympic rules.

The fourth-century B.C. philosopher Aristotle once compared a fight between armed and unarmed men with a contest between 'athletes' and 'non-professionals' (*idiotai*). The Greek word *idiotes* had an extended range of meanings—civilian, private citizen, non-professional, ignoramus (from which our 'idiot' is ultimately descended). For Aristotle it was as absurd for an unarmed man to fight an armed man as for an amateur to compete with a professional athlete. 'Professional' to him, as to every Greek, meant a man who received proper training and devoted himself more or less full-time to an activity; an *idiotes* (we should say 'an amateur') did neither. The modern distinction—whether or not one was paid for the activity—did not enter into the picture for the simple reason that all athletes expected and accepted material rewards for victory, regardless of class or personal fortune. It is a modern falsification of the ancient record to link the rise of professional athletics with the decline in the aristocratic monopoly. We have already seen that even Homer's noblemen competed for expensive prizes on some occasions. Then in the first phase of the Circuit and of the growing number of local prize Games, well-trained and coached aristocrats dominated, becoming the first professional athletes in European (and perhaps world) history.

They could afford to take on this new role, because their families had the means with which to hire the best trainers and coaches, to insure a proper diet, with plenty of meat, to support them financially until they were ready to retire from competition, which was sometimes not much before the age of forty. If they had Olympic ambitions, there were the further costs of travel and of the ten months of full-time training beforehand and of the obligatory month in Elis. For obvious reasons, the wealthier classes retained a monopoly of the equestrian events to the end. They need have no skill whatever in horsemanship, but they had to possess a sufficient fortune with which to pay for horses and stables, grooms and jockeys, and to transport animals, gear and personnel to the Games, adding up to one of the most expensive tastes known to the ancient world. Hence the list of 'winners' runs from early tyrants or Athenian noblemen like Miltiades, uncle of the general of the same name who won the battle of Marathon, through Philip II of Macedon, father of Alexander the Great (who himself had weightier matters on his mind), and a number of Hellenistic monarchs, down to Nero or the third-century A.D. Athenian magnate, T. Domitius Prometheus.

No poor or even middle-class boy could dream of an equestrian victory, except as a hired jockey. But all the other events gradually became open to him; if he showed championship promise, his ambition was encouraged by his native city, which provided the cash he and his family lacked. There were occasional private patrons, and under the Roman Empire the newly created associations of professional athletes sometimes helped, too, but basically it was a matter of the generous outlay of public funds. The largest share went into the construction and maintenance of public gymnasia, a pivotal institution as we shall see in the next chapter. But the gymnasium became the headquarters of the 'gilded youth' of the cities. No son of a shopkeeper or craftsman, let alone a peasant, was free to spend enough of his time there or to equip himself properly. Direct subsidies were essential.

If successful in the long training period, the athlete then had to be supported in his professional career, and that, too, depended on the city, which either sponsored Games itself, paying for the costs and for the prizes, or supplemented the token prizes won by its own victors in other Games with hard cash, or did both. Many boys of course failed to make the grade and dropped out. Aristotle, who favoured physical education for the young but believed that intensive early specialization had harmful effects, observed that his views were confirmed by the lists of Olympic victors, which revealed that very few who won in a boys' event went on to succeed in the men's

competition. Boy winners were sufficiently honoured, but it was the
men who mattered most, and who in the end were a considerable
expense to so many Greek communities. The number of Games increased steadily, the opportunities for professional athletes grew
apace, so did their numbers and so did the costs.

We mentioned earlier, in connection with the financing of the
Olympic Games, that 'public funds' in this kind of activity commonly
included a charge levied directly on the wealthier citizens, not on the
treasury as we would understand it. Civic pride was their reward,
and nothing was more likely to win them wide popularity, and therefore political authority as well. The traditional Greek love of competition triumphed over other values: in Athens, the most democratic
of all Greek cities, the aristocratic Alcibiades could trade on his
spectacular record in the Olympic chariot race of 416 to gain political
advantage, while in even the most fiercely oligarchic cities the ruling
families were happy, for their own glory and their city's, to help
finance and develop potential winners from those classes in society
whom they otherwise held in contempt and in a state of political
impotence.

In short, after the initial era of aristocratic monopoly, professional
athletics became and remained 'classless'. There was no democratiza-
tion of sport in general: most boys and young men had no opportunity
to engage in athletics as a normal part of their leisure-time activity.
At the Games level, however, the competitors were drawn from every
social stratum in the Greek cities, training, travelling and contesting
together on equal terms. No statistics are possible. Unless a bit of
personal information happens to survive, we cannot determine today
whether any given Olympic victor came from the highest or the
lowest social circles. We cannot even assert that bribery and other
forms of corruption were more likely to have involved athletes from
underprivileged backgrounds. Nor is the familiar modern saying, that
only hunger produces great boxers (as an example), applicable.
Theogenes of Thasos in the fifth century B.C. and Nicophon of
Miletus in the first are proof enough. The wrestler with 127 victories,

[73]

mentioned at the beginning of this chapter, was a certain M. Aurelius Hermagoras, from a little town in Asia Minor, whose family included several high magistrates of his native city, a sure sign at that time of wealth and social standing. Yet his was also a wrestling family: the father was an Olympic victor in A.D. 137.

How much did such a champion earn in his career, or the many less successful athletes who won only occasionally? (Anyone who could never win the first, and only, prize would soon enough be compelled to abandon an athletic career, unless he had independent means.) The direct answer is that there is no way of knowing. Whenever the athletes speak themselves, in the inscriptions recording their triumphs (Plate 2b) or in documents issued by their professional associations (Plate 26), money is never mentioned. Nor is it in the early choral odes in their honour or in official honorary decrees (Plate 24a). But there are clues. The 30,000-drachma 'fee' paid to an Olympic victor as the price for his appearance in a local Games festival must represent an upper limit. The second-century A.D. prize table from Aphrodisias, ranging from 500 drachmas in the pentathlon to 3000 in the pankration, was fairly representative for its time. That ranked Aphrodisias among the 3000-drachma Games, as they were commonly labelled. Richer ones were 6000-drachma Games. These are large sums, as the comparison we drew earlier with a soldier's pay illuminates.

The availability of large prizes and special fees strengthened the need for athletes to publicize their achievements. The accounts that have come down to us are mostly summaries made public after or near retirement, but outstanding records were surely made known, where it mattered, while a man was still fit for further competition and further rewards. Besides, what they said at the end of a career just as accurately reflected their values and those of their patrons and supporters. Some modern historians have taken a cynical view of these documents, without warrant. We cannot check the details, to be sure, but they reveal nuances and a discrimination that do not sound like mere public relations. No one is likely to have invented such a figure as 127 for the total of his victories. Nor could anyone

PLATE 17 The 'heave' in wrestling: two scenes showing Theseus about to defeat the famous legendary wrestler, Cercyon of Arcadia, at Eleusis on the outskirts of Athens. Theseus was the Athenian local 'hero': son of the king of Athens, he was brought up in Troezen in the Peloponnese, which he left when he had attained manhood, proceeded to Athens on foot and had a series of 'heroic' adventures on the way. The encounter with the wrestler Cercyon, whom he killed after he had defeated him, became the favourite wrestling theme among Athenian sculptors and vase painters. (For another wrestling scene, see the neck of the vase in Plate 20.)

(a) A detail from a rather cracked Athenian red-figured cup of the late sixth century B.C.

(b) One of the sculptured scenes over the east portico of the Hephaesteum (see Plate 8b).

PLATE 18 (a) The Stadium at Olympia as it appears today, seen from the northeast (see Figs. 7-10). The length is about 214 m overall, 192 m between the starting- and finishing-lines. The shaded rectangle on the left of the Stadium towards the farther end is the judges' stand (Fig. 4), which was, curiously enough, about one third of the way along the course. There were no seats for spectators, just as there were none at Delphi until late in the second century A.D. (see Plate 19 opposite). The athletes entered through a tunnel at the far right-hand corner of the Stadium.

(b) The grooved sills which served as the starting-line for races at the Isthmian Games (one of the four 'Circuit' Games. See p. 23). The postholes, 25 cm deep and lined with lead, for the starting-gates can be seen. There was space for sixteen gates in all.

(c) A reconstruction of the starting-gates. The gates were controlled by strings running in the grooves to the central starting-pit in the foreground of (b). This reconstruction is by O. Broneer.

PLATE 19 (a) The Stadium at Delphi as it appears today. It lies in a spectacular position on the slopes of Mt. Parnassus, which rises a further 250 m above it. It was constructed in the second half of the fifth century B.C. above the sacred precinct with the famous theatre and high above the valley floor. Earlier races were held in the Hippodrome lower down. The Stadium was laid out on a rock terrace cut into the face of the mountain and supported by massive foundations. The distance between the starting- and finishing-lines is 177·5 m and the width 28·5 m at the centre, slightly smaller than at Olympia. The grooved marble starting-slabs are clearly visible at the nearer end, and are comparable to those at Olympia (for a different layout, see Plate 18b and c). For centuries there were no seats, except for the judges halfway down the northern, left-hand, side. What we now see is the work of Herodes Atticus in the second half of the second century A.D., who was also a major benefactor to Olympia (see p. 52 and Plate 30d). The four pillars at the far end held a triumphal arch, built at the same time to provide a ceremonial entrance for the officials and competitors.

(b) A view of Nemea, showing three columns of the temple of Zeus. This site is the poorest of the four 'Circuit' precincts in its archaeological remains, with scarcely a trace of the Games.

PLATE 20 This scene shows one boxer bleeding from the nose, and, in the neck of the vase, two wrestlers (see also Plate 17). The amphora was made and signed by a well known potter, Nicosthenes, in the second half of the sixth century B.C. Despite the Panathenaic shape, this amphora was not intended to be a prize for a victor, since the other side does not have the figure of Athena. Instead it has a similar double scene with the wrestlers on the body and the boxers on the neck.

PLATE 21 This scene gives a clear picture of the thong-bindings of the boxers' hands, and suggests the magnificent physique of the contestants. The figure at the left of the picture is completing, with his teeth, the fastening of his thong-bindings. This amphora is one of the few with a date inscribed on it, in this case 336/5 B.C., the first year of the reign of Alexander the Great. By this time the black-figured technique had been largely abandoned in Athens for about a century and a half—its retention for Panathenaic amphoras is typical of the conservatism in matters relating to the major Games (see also Plate IV). It was found in an Etruscan tomb at Cerveteri.

PLATE 22 Two scenes of the pankration (from the Greek adjective, *pankrates*, 'all-powerful'), the favourite sport of all at Olympia, which may be described as a combination of wrestling and judo, with boxing—almost 'no holds barred'.
(a) In this picture the lower pankratiast is conceding defeat by tapping his opponent on the shoulder. The judge's whip is visible in the upper right-hand corner. This is on an Athenian cup of the late sixth century B.C.

(b) In this scene the pankratiasts are on the right. One is trying to gouge his opponent's eye, an illegal action causing the trainer to bring his whip into play. On the wall behind hangs a bag for a discus. The figures at the left are boxers. This is also on an Athenian cup, of the fifth century B.C.

PLATE 23   GREEK SILVER COINS (2½–3 times actual size)

(a) Nike (the goddess Victory) flies to crown the victorious horses of Gelon, tyrant of Gela, who won the chariot race at the Olympic Games in 488 B.C. and became tyrant of Syracuse in 485 B.C. A tetradrachm from Syracuse, issued about 485 B.C.

(b) Tetradrachm from Rhegium in southern Italy, issued to commemorate the victory of Anaxilas, tyrant of that city, in the Olympic mule-cart race of 480 B.C.

(c) Wrestlers on a stater (didrachm) from Aspendus in Asia Minor, early fourth century B.C.

(d) Discus-thrower on a tridrachm from the island of Cos, mid-fifth century B.C.

PLATE 24 (a) A stone inscription from Didyma, one of the great oracle-shrines of Apollo, in the territory of Miletus, dating from the third century A.D. The inscription reads: 'The council and people have honoured Aurelius Synekdemos, victor in the boys' wrestling at the Great Didymeia, when Aelianus Poplas was prophet (keeper of the oracle). The statue was erected when Aurelius Apphianos was a prophet.' Of the three designs at the bottom of the stone, the one in the left corner represents the victor's laurel wreath, the central one the metal urn from which the draw was made (see Plate 24c), the one at the right a decoration added solely for the sake of symmetry. (The photograph is taken from a squeeze of the stone in Paris and the letters and design therefore appear as if moulded rather than incised.)

(b) A seat of blue-black marble, found at Olympia in the area of the early Stadium. The inscription round the rim reads: 'Gorgos the Lacedaemonian, *proxenos* of the Eleans.' 'Lacedaemonian' was a common synonym for 'Spartan'; a *proxenos* was a citizen of city A (in this case Sparta) who helped citizens of city B (Elis) when they were in city A, somewhat in the manner of a modern consul. Gorgos is otherwise unknown, but *proxenoi* were normally men of high social standing, and often of political standing too. The style of lettering is that of Sparta, not of Elis, of the first half of the sixth century B.C. The stonecutter stood the marble upright and carved the inscription from right to left, so that it has to be read 'from the inside'. The seat is 38 cm × 31 cm.

(c) Three naked athletes drawing from an urn to determine either their positions in a race or the draw in boxing or a similar event. A bronze coin (about twice actual size) from Ancyra (modern Ankara), capital of the Roman province of Galatia. The inscription reads: 'Equal-Pythian Games [in honour] of the Healer-God Asclepius [organized] by the Capital Ancyra'. These Games were either founded or raised to 'equal-Pythian' rank (see p. 111) by permission of the emperor Caracalla (198-217), whose head appears on the other side of the coin, at the time of his protracted illness in Asia Minor in A.D. 214 while he was at war with the Parthians.

have falsely claimed a Circuit victory when the official lists were available for scrutiny.

If we had in our possession all the texts that were inscribed and posted in one place or another for a thousand years, we could produce a veritable *Guinness Book of Records*. We would not know who ran the fastest 200 metres or made the longest discus throw. Such records were never kept. Instead, we should have a catalogue of 'quality records', so to speak. In addition to the boxers who were 'never wounded', the wrestlers who were never brought to their knees or never defeated, the men who won without opposition, all mentioned earlier, there were the curious winners 'without having drawn a bye', that is to say, having had to fight in every round or race in every heat because of the luck of the draw. A little imagination could stretch the field for such claims a long way: one great pankratiast of the end of the second century A.D. required ten lines (before he got down to listing his victories) in order to enumerate his 'nevers', which included never having asked permission to withdraw and never having competed in a 'new' Game.

Another theme and variations developed round the boast of having been the first to achieve something. Theogenes of Thasos was acclaimed as the first man to win both in boxing and the pankration on the same day (at the Isthmian Games), to win both events in the Olympics (in successive Games, having abandoned an earlier effort to accomplish that on a single day), and to score three successive boxing victories in major Games (at the Pythian Games, once without opposition). A contemporary of his, Xenophon of Corinth, won the sprint and the pentathlon in the same Olympiad: 'He has won what no mortal man has won before', wrote Pindar in his victory ode, and then, in the Pythian Games, 'he has the glory of the foot-race and the double-race in a single sun', followed by a triple win at the Panathenaic Games 'in the same moon'. Others were driven to lesser claims, such as 'the first of the Rhodians' to gain victories in two successive Olympics, or 'the first of the Greeks from Asia', and so on. Even youngsters chimed in: a Hellenistic epigram celebrates an

[75]

ephebe's double victory on the same day, in boxing and the pankration, in contests in his local gymnasium on the island of Thera (modern Santorini). The epigram is addressed to the patrons of the gymnasium, Hermes and Heracles.

It will be observed that in our Book of Records, Theogenes' entries are less impressive for the Olympic Games than for the rest of the Circuit. Yet he named his son Twice-Olympian ('Disolympios' in Greek). That was in the mid-fifth century B.C., and the primacy of Olympia remained unshaken in the more elaborate 'bookkeeping' of Roman imperial times, many centuries later. In these accounts the athletes usually gave only the raw total of their victories in prize Games, without naming any of them, regularly specified the Circuit prizes, and almost always listed Olympia first if they had won there some time or other in their careers.* Or, as had not been the case earlier, they now boasted of an Olympic draw, even of 'having fought for the wreath', which implies having reached the finals and then lost. Boys were sometimes said 'to have been admitted and to have participated'. The absence of any reference to the Olympic Games was a silent admission of failure. When a second-century pankratiast who had 21 wins in sacred Games and 36 in prize Games begins his catalogue with his triumph at the relatively new 'Olympic' Games in Athens, we can be certain that he never won the real Olympics, and that is confirmed by his inclusion of draws in the Nemean and Isthmian Games. We can be equally certain that a professional of that calibre would have tried for the olive wreath at some time in his career, unless he scratched in order to avoid likely defeat.

So Olympia could hold fast to its ancient rule of awarding no material prizes. Other sacred Games, with a lesser appeal, eventually had to make a direct concession to the professionals, at least by the time there were several hundred Games to compete in. Olympia was one of the few which could refuse: we remember the boxer who in A.D. 93 was so enraged by his exclusion for late arrival that he

* An occasional exception was made for victory in the Games of one's native city, which might be named ahead of Olympia.

punched the winner during the award ceremony. The Olympic Games promised the greatest glory and fame—we should not underestimate that side of professional athletics—and they also enhanced a competitor's market-value. A 30,000-drachma fee may have been exceptional; more modest inducements to attract champions to lesser prize Games would have been common.

From a surprisingly early date, cities also began to supplement the token prizes of the sacred Games. Homecoming celebrations, with processions a regular feature (the ancient version of the modern ticker-tape parade), were valued and maintained, but cash and goods were not less attractive. Early in the sixth century B.C. the Athenian lawgiver and constitutional reformer, Solon, is said to have introduced a scale of bonuses for Athenian victors, ranging from 500 drachmas for the Olympics to 100 for the Isthmian Games. This is puzzling, and our ancient authorities (all much later than Solon) were themselves agreed neither on the precise arrangements nor on Solon's motives. He was certainly not thinking that early about potential Athenian champions from lower-class families: for at least two centuries after Solon not a single Athenian Olympic victor is recorded who did not belong to the highest social stratum. However, there must be a hard core of truth in the tradition. A recently discovered contemporary text from Sybaris, a Greek colony in southern Italy, reveals that an Olympic victor from that city, legendary for its wealth, had spent one tenth of his prize, a tithe in other words, on a statue (or shrine) to a local goddess. 'His prize' could mean only the money Sybaris had awarded him for his Olympic triumph. By 300 B.C. Ephesus had statutorily fixed cash awards (of unknown amounts) for the Circuit wreaths, apparently different for each of the Games. And these cities we have mentioned are only examples of a widespread development.

Gradually, as professional athletics spread to the lower classes, this practice amounted in effect to yet another addition to the ever-increasing pool of money for which the professionals competed. Sacred Games thus joined the ranks of prize Games in a roundabout way. Another honour underwent a similar transformation: the traditional privilege of free dinners in the town-hall was sometimes converted into a pension for a fixed period and even for life, paid monthly, and delicately posted under the heading of 'rations' in the municipal accounts. By the early Hellenistic period, municipal budgets regularly included sums earmarked for 'public creditors, priests and victors in sacred Games', and there was, city by city, a standardized cash value for each prize and each pension. From the late third century A.D. we hear of a boxer who claimed two pensions, each of 180 drachmas a month. And fixed-term pensions were a 'property': they could be sold or transmitted by inheritance.

The fiscal drain was not negligible. Hermopolis on the Nile is known to have paid out some 50,000 drachmas in a single year late in the third century A.D. Such a figure suggests that even the Roman emperors, who expressed dismay over outlays of that scale from the beginning of the imperial period, were fairly powerless in the matter. The problem had its amusing side, too, when a storm arose over the perquisites of victors in the so-called 'triumphal Games'. It was a very old tradition that a Circuit winner was entitled to a triumphal entry into his native city in a four-horse chariot, though not many would have gone so far as luxury-loving Acragas (modern Agrigento) in Sicily when it welcomed its Olympic 200-metre champion, Exaenetus, in 412 B.C.: 'He was conducted into the city in a chariot, and in the procession there were three hundred chariots each drawn by a pair of white horses, all the property of citizens of Acragas.' By Roman times, more and more of the sacred Games had acquired 'triumphal' standing, with a consequent increase in the costs of celebrations and pensions. The emperors, in an effort to regularize the situation and also to dampen the exuberance, claimed the right to award or withdraw the 'triumphal' title. The athletes naturally resisted, seizing any available opening.

A direct conflict arose in Bithynia (in Asia Minor) early in the second century: the athletes claimed that their pension rights began on the day of victory, also that they should be given retrospective benefits for winning in Games declared at a later date to be 'triumphal'. The emperor, Trajan, rejected both demands. A triumph, he argued, must be understood literally, and therefore it could not begin until the triumphal re-entry. As for retrospective payments, no one was asked to return a pension when Games were subsequently downgraded, and the athletes must take the swings with the roundabouts.

This particular squabble may seem little more than hair-splitting. However, at the rates of reward we have already noticed, the sums involved were not paltry, apart from the larger issues of control at stake. Not only was there a saving for the time it took to return from Olympia, for example, to Asia Minor, but there was the possibility of further saving if the champion continued on his tour of Games before coming home. That was now the normal routine of such professionals.

They were not alone in this way of life. It must be remembered that Games normally included musical and theatrical competitions, also the province of a group of professionals who toured constantly. Not later than 300 B.C. the latter had formed an Association of Dionysiac Artists, and it is one of our frustrating puzzles that we cannot trace a similar association among the athletes earlier than about 50 B.C. The organization of members of a single occupation or profession into societies was a feature of the Greek world from the Hellenistic period on. Historians commonly refer to them by their Latin name, *collegia*, rather than as 'guilds' or 'trades unions', because they were social, benevolent and religious societies with little or no strictly economic function, whatever the material side-effects may have been. Each city had its own *collegia*, which did not combine in larger territorial federations. The actors and athletes constituted an exception precisely because their activity was 'world-wide'.

No doubt the top professional athletes residing in such a sporting centre as Ephesus or Alexandria had long had some sort of local social association, and perhaps the athletes were content for a time to join the Association of Dionysiac Artists. In the end, however, they adopted the obvious course and organized themselves; in fact, they seem originally to have had two associations, one open to everyone who toured professionally, the other restricted to men who had scored a victory in one of the sacred Games. Then, probably not long before A.D. 150, the two merged permanently and moved their headquarters from somewhere in the East to the city of Rome, in order to have quick and easy access to the imperial court.

The officers of the association were chosen from their own ranks (we do not know how): not only such self-evident ones as president, secretary, and treasurer, but also the priests, whether as a permanent duty in the association's headquarters in Rome or as a temporary one for one of the Games in the Greek east, the honorand paying (*not* being paid) a fee for the privilege (Plate 26). Occupational associations normally had a patron deity to whom they sacrificed, and the athletes not surprisingly chose Heracles. Sometimes the name of the society, as it appears in an ancient document, actually includes the words 'those associated with Heracles'. The addition of an emperor's name or two as patron was no sign of disrespect to Heracles; it was merely a recognition of the benefits to be gained, or hoped for, from a favourably inclined emperor, such as exemption for the association's members from municipal taxes, military service or the compulsory billeting of soldiers, or the privilege of supervising Games on behalf of the emperors, who, largely for fiscal reasons, wished to keep an eye on both sacred and prize Games—but never the Olympic Games or the other most ancient sacred Games.

It is necessary to add at once that the day-to-day activity of the association, or of the two before their merger, cannot be properly characterized by concentrating on their involvement with emperors. Mostly there was routine activity, the sacrifices and feasts, funerals when necessary; concern with amenities, travel arrangements and the scale of prizes; a check on the timetable, so that members were not frustrated by too many competing Games; the persistent pursuit of honours for individual members, from cities and officials or from the association itself. Typical is a memorial decree issued by the association of all athletes honouring the memory of a colleague from Asia

Minor who had died young. He is praised for 'his nobility and the generosity of his ancestors', a stereotyped formula to be sure, revealing the high social standing of the young man, but not a meaningless formula. Generosity was what made the very existence of the professional athletes possible; they knew it and they said so openly.

Membership was open to every qualified athlete regardless of social or regional origin within the Empire. Trainers also belonged, presumably having joined in their youth as practising athletes. Even the attainment of offices and other honours depended in large part, though not wholly, on athletic success rather than on other, extraneous considerations. The situation is beautifully summed up in a papyrus of the end of the second century, the 'membership certificate' of an Egyptian boxer named Herminus, which indicates the records of a number of officials and also exposes the extent of their education (Plate 26). The famous pankratiast and 'invincible' boxer, M. Aurelius Demostratus Damas of Sardis, one of the association's high priests, honorary citizen of ten cities, twice victor in the pankration in all four of the Circuit Games, wrote correct Greek in a good hand. His son, we know from another source, held the highest public office in their native Sardis. But two of the presidents of the association, both from Asia Minor and both Olympic victors, one in boxing, the other in running, wrote ungrammatical and barely literate Greek. Herminus himself could scarcely sign his name, yet he was once designated by the association as its representative and priest, on payment of a fee of fifty denarii, at 'the Sacred Triumphal World Games held in Sardis by the Federation of the Province of Asia'.

Such men could not possibly have started life among the 'gilded youth' who made the gymnasia their headquarters. Their athletic successes raised their social status, won them a variety of honours and substantial wealth. What did they do when age forced them to retire from their profession, by the time they were forty or even sooner? If they lacked inherited wealth and had not saved enough from their winnings on which to live comfortably, buttressed by municipal pensions, they were qualified for one occupation alone, that of trainer, for the ancient economy was not one in which they could be an asset to a business solely (or largely) because of their reputation and their contacts. Otherwise, they could occupy themselves with the management of games or with politics, if the circumstances were right. These are among the things we shall look at in the following chapters.

7

Training and Trainers

Early in the second century B.C., in the bitter days of Antiochus Epiphanes, the ruling aristocracy in Judaea, led by Jason the high priest, embarked on a programme of Hellenization. They were 'wicked men', thundered the author of 1 Maccabees, 'who persuaded many, saying "Let us go and make a covenant with the Gentiles that are round about us". . . . Whereupon they built a gymnasium in Jerusalem according to the custom of the Gentiles.' Nothing was more typically, and quintessentially, Greek by that time than a gymnasium.

Our word 'gymnasium', like 'stadium', though Greek in origin, has specific connotations which give a false picture if read back mechanically to antiquity. The ancient institution, the introduction of which can be dated to the early sixth century B.C., was a complex of buildings and open spaces designed to fulfil several different functions. One of these, physical training and practice in the various sports in which Greeks indulged (a more numerous assortment than the few included in Games), was the dominant one—hence the meaning of the word in English—but it was neither the only one nor the original one. Although the first gymnasia we can trace were erected in precisely the period when both the Games Circuit and ordinary prize Games were

[83]

being established, there is good reason to believe that the main impetus came from military developments. When the nobility lost its military predominance and near-monopoly to the massed infantry phalanx, the community was faced for the first time with the problem of training a proportion of its young men in the requisite military skills, and of keeping them fit for service after the initial training period. These were for the most part men who, though rich enough to equip themselves with arms and armour, the sons of more prosperous farmers or owners of urban establishments, were a different breed from the old warrior aristocracy, for whom war, hunting and sports had been the way of life.

Wrestling, boxing, running, javelin-throwing, the pankration and the rest were all easily conceived as ideal ways of preparing young men for armed hand-to-hand combat. Hence the gymnasium included exercise-rooms with punching-bags and other equipment (Figs. 13 and 14), baths and grounds not unlike those at Olympia for outdoor sports and drills, in time also gardens, parks, perhaps a library

Fig. 13 A dwarf practising the pankration by kicking a punching bag made of a stuffed pig's skin. Caricature from an Athenian vase of the late fifth century B.C.

Fig. 14 Athletes exercising and practising in a gymnasium (from an
Athenian red-figured bowl of the late sixth century B.C.).

(Plate 28). Sparta found gymnasia unnecessary, since military training
was the exclusive occupation of all citizen males from the age of seven.
Olympia, too, managed without one (in the formal sense) until quite
late (see Fig. 9), but for a different reason, namely, that Olympia was
not a community and had no young men of its own to train. But
otherwise the gymnasium rapidly became a feature of all Greek cities,
and, so long as these cities remained independent political units with
their own armies, the military side remained important. Then, after
Alexander the Great and the creation of the Hellenistic monarchies,

full-time professional armies more or less destroyed that function of the gymnasia, although a nostalgic link with the military was retained. Now the gymnastic and athletic functions became ends in themselves quite openly, as they had to an extent been all the time tacitly, with competitions the norm and Games the final goal for the best of the athletes.

Surprisingly, to us at least, there was still a third function. We mentioned at the beginning of this book that philosophers and itinerant orators lectured in the gymnasia. In fact, genuine institutions of higher education were sometimes located there. The most spectacular instances occurred in Athens, where the three oldest and most celebrated gymnasia, all in the suburbs, were known as the Academy, the Lyceum and the Cynosarges. Early in the fourth century B.C. Plato established his school at the Academy; later in the same century Aristotle followed suit at the Lyceum, and then Diogenes began to teach at the Cynosarges (hence he and his disciples came to be known as Cynics).

We need not imagine that aspiring military commanders or Olympic winners interrupted their training to study philosophy under Plato or Aristotle. Yet the fact remains that gymnasia were thought of, in the words of a young Asia Minor athlete about 100 B.C., as centres of training 'for the body and the soul', different as the relative proportions may have been among those who frequented them. Plato, in an early dialogue, the *Meno*, has Socrates comment disingenuously, but not inaccurately, in the course of an inquiry whether virtue can be taught or not, that Pericles, 'that great and wise man', failed to make his two sons 'good men' despite the fact that he 'had them taught riding, music, athletics and all the other skilled pursuits till they were as good at them as any in Athens'. It is a fine historical irony that 'academy' and 'lyceum' survive as modern words only in their pedagogical sense (and that in Germany, for example, 'gymnasium' is to this day the generic name for the most academic type of secondary school).

Finally, the gymnasium also had a place for religion. That hardly needs comment: no Greek centre, public or private, could exist without its accompanying cult activity. Nor is it necessary to elaborate on the fact that the cult of Heracles was especially prominent.

It was all this, not physical exercise of itself, that aroused the indignation of the majority of Palestinian Jews, for whom the author of 1 Maccabees was a spokesman, and the bewilderment, at the very least, of the other nationalities among whom the eastern Greeks lived ever since Alexander's conquests. In particular, they rebelled against the nakedness and the pederasty that were inseparable from the Greek gymnasium (much as modern apologists may seek to ignore these features). 'Pederasty' is to be understood in its root-sense in Greek, erotic love of adult males for adolescent boys (Plate 31b).

In the days of the independent city with its citizen militia, able-bodied young men with the requisite property qualification were normally required to undergo military training when they were eighteen and nineteen. They came to be known as *ephebes*, and the label clung after the military side became increasingly an anachronism, after attendance ceased to be compulsory and became instead a rather expensive privilege. The ephebes were to the end the fashionable 'gilded youth' of the Greek cities, the gymnasium was their home, athletics and games their central activity (Plates 22b, 29). Naturally they did not all abandon this overriding interest on reaching the age of twenty. For many adults whose means gave them the requisite leisure, the gymnasium continued to be the main social centre (and boys younger than eighteen were eventually admitted, too). There future Games winners were bred and fostered, and there close ties were forged, within the same age-group and between young and adult, erotic but also potentially valuable as social and political connections.

In the early days of the gymnasium, the traditional aristocratic families were faced with an acute social problem. Should they come in or stay out? The former entailed recognition of the upstart families now claiming their place in the world of athletics and Games, as they had already won a place in the armies. The latter meant risking their chance for the prizes in the Games, the cash awards as well as the wreaths. They could not expect to compete indefinitely on an equal basis with the boys and men who had become professionals under the guidance of professional trainers and coaches. They resisted the hard choice, no doubt, but in the end they capitulated. From the late fourth century B.C., the gymnasium became an institution for the 'gilded youth', a cross-section of the richer strata of the population, regardless of ancestry and family tradition, and that is what it remained to the end of antiquity.

The gymnasium also created the first opportunity for promising poor boys to try for an athletic career, though the precise mechanics are not very clear to us. No doubt their ambition would not for some time have reached beyond local Games, simply because of the high costs of participation at the Circuit level, the costs of travel and maintenance during the compulsory training-period, and, before that, the special training and care, the freedom to devote all one's time to athletics, requisite for competition at top level. The gymnasium, in short, was a necessary condition for the new social phenomenon of lower-class Olympic champions, but it was not a sufficient condition. Indeed, neither was it a sufficient condition for champions of any social background, and that requires further consideration.*

It is essential to grasp that the gymnasium was a public institution, built and administered by the municipal authorities. As always, private contributions towards the costs were welcomed and indeed solicited. For Hellenistic kings, Roman emperors and other great men with large fortunes, the gymnasium became one of the favourite objects of benefactions. But even they made their gifts for this purpose to the city itself. Increasingly, the official in charge, usually but not always called 'gymnasiarch', was also expected to be open-handed on a considerable scale. And once the cities lost their political autonomy,

* Perhaps it should be said explicitly that slaves were excluded from the gymnasia except as attendants. According to the ancient dream interpreters, if a slave dreamed that he was exercising in a gymnasium (or that he had won an Olympic wreath), it meant that he would soon be freed.

the office of gymnasiarch climbed the honorific ladder and often became the highest post a man could fill within the limited world of municipal affairs (Fig. 15).

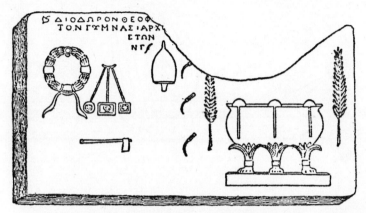

Fig. 15 Tombstone of Diodorus, son of Theoph . . ., gymnasiarch, who died at the age of fifty-three. Engraved on the stone from left to right are a wreath, three tablets each containing a portrait-head, below an axe, an unidentified object, three strigils (scrapers), and, flanked by two palms, a large, ornate oil-tank with three ladles. The tank symbolizes both the large quantities of oil consumed in the gymnasia and the financial contribution expected of the gymnasiarch towards the cost. This tombstone, of dimensions 1.57 × 0.83 m, is from the Roman period and was found at Prusa, in northwestern Asia Minor.

The gymnasiarch was a civic functionary, not a specialist in physical education or sports. That role was taken by professional trainers who were employed by the city; the stress on 'employed' is critical, reflecting the great divide between the gymnasiarch and the trainer. The latter, usually a retired athlete, was expected to be expert in all branches of his profession, from the lowly masseur (one Greek word commonly used for 'trainer', *aleiptes*, means just that) to dietitian, physiotherapist and hygienist and on to coach in our sense, the man who instructs in the actual techniques of wrestling, boxing, sprinting or jumping (Fig. 16). In scenes on painted pottery, the

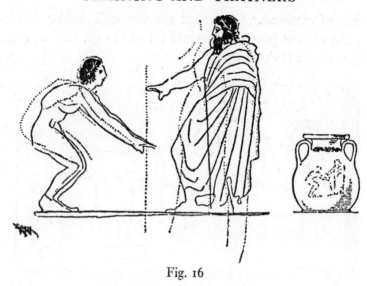

Fig. 16

trainer (as we shall call him in all his functions) is shown clothed, with the inevitable whip at the ready (Plate 14), but he was expected to strip at a moment's notice in order to give a demonstration of the finer points of a racing start or a pankration hold.

There was of course nothing to prevent men of wealth from owning personal rooms or even buildings for physical training,* or individual trainers from setting themselves up privately in their own athletic schools. The passage from Plato's *Meno* we have quoted earlier goes on to give another example of a father's failure to train his sons in virtue: a political opponent of Pericles', the oligarchically inclined Thucydides son of Melesias, gave his two sons 'an excellent education. Among other things they were the best wrestlers in Athens, for he gave one to Xanthias to train and the other to Eudoxus, the two men who, I understand, were considered the finest wrestlers of their time'. For the first half of that (fifth) century, Pindar, who was never ironic on this subject, names five private trainers of the aristocratic victors he was celebrating, all in body-contact sports. And his language is

* A private establishment was usually called palaestra, not gymnasium, but the Greek language was loose, so that there were also public palaestras, as at Olympia.

PLATE 25 The record of an Athenian wrestler and pankratiast, Menodorus, the greatest champion of his day. This is the marble base (190 cm by 96 cm) of a life-sized statue (now lost) of Menodorus dedicated about 135-130 B.C. to Apollo on the island of Delos, where there was the most important pan-Hellenic shrine of the god after Delphi. Another side of the base, not shown, inscribed with the name of the man who made the dedication, Demetrius, son of Apollodotus, who is otherwise unknown, describes Menodorus as 'victor in the Circuit and the other sacred Games'. All but the last four wreaths commemorate victories: the type of event is given within the wreath, the Games are identified above it, and the stonecutter made a crude, but unsuccessful, attempt to distinguish the wreaths. Of the total of 32 victories, 18 were in the pankration, 14 in wrestling (two of these in boys' competitions). The third from the left in the top row is the Olympic wreath for wrestling, the fourth from the left in the third row the Olympic wreath for the pankration. There were five victories in his native Athens, five in the Games at Thebes in honour of Heracles, three Nemean victories, and the others scattered about Greece. The absence of an Isthmian victory presumably reflects a period when these Games were not held following the destruction of Corinth by the Romans in 146 B.C. The last four wreaths in the final line mark not victories but honours given to Menodorus by Athens, Rhodes, Thebes and King Ariarathes V of Cappadocia in Asia Minor (who died about 130 B.C.). Fragments of a sculptured group honouring him have also been found in the central square, the Agora, of Athens.

PLATE 26 The opening and closing sections of the 'membership certificate' of the boxer Herminus in the Sacred Hadrian Antoninus Septimius Association of Touring Athletes, issued in Naples on 23 September A.D. 194. (See the closing pages of Chapter 6.)

The 'certificate' takes the form of a letter to the members of the Association. The opening lines read as follows:

'Herminus, known as Moros, boxer from Hermopolis.

'The Sacred Hadrian Antoninus Septimius Association of Touring Athletes to the members of that Association: Greetings. Be it known that Herminus, known as Moros, a boxer from Hermopolis, aged [figure missing], is one of our members and has paid in full the statutory entrance fee, 100 denarii. We write to you so that you shall know. Farewell.'

The final nineteen lines, reproduced in the second picture, are attestations of Herminus' priesthood in the association. They begin:

'I, Photion son of Karpion, from Laodicea, honorary citizen of Ephesus, boxing victor in the Olympic Games, wrestler, distinguished athlete, President of the Sacred Association of Touring Athletes, witness by my signature that Herminus, known as Moros, from Hermopolis, served in my presence as priest at the Sacred Triumphal World Games held in Sardis by the Federation of the Province of Asia. 50 denarii.'

The second deposition, in virtually the identical words, is by another president, a runner from the city of Philadelphia in Asia Minor, honorary citizen of Ephesus and Tralles, also an Olympic victor. Shorter statements follow, signed by the treasurer of the association; by the high priest, a native of Sardis, whose impressive record, given in detail earlier in the document, includes honorary citizenship of Alexandria, Athens, Miletus and Sparta, among other cities, and victory twice in the pankration in all four Games in the Circuit; and by the secretary.

The papyrus roll, about one metre in length and containing 102 lines of text, was found in the ruins of Herminus' native town, Great Hermopolis, on the Nile a little more than 200 kilometres south of Memphis. It was first published in 1907 in *Greek Papyri in the British Museum*, vol. 3. The papyrus is about 24 cm wide—in the first picture it is reduced by 40 per cent and in the second by 70 per cent.

PLATE 27 A decree of the Acarnanian League, probably in 216 B.C., agreeing to assume responsibility for rebuilding the temple of Apollo at Actium and re-establishing the annual Games there. The shrine and Games had been in the charge of the city of Anactoria, in whose territory Actium was located, but a period of intense warfare had brought the Games to a halt and the shrine into a bad state of disrepair. Anactoria was financially unable to take on the task of reconstruction, hence the intervention of the League, which promised to organize the Games annually, as in the past, unless further war interfered. Two copies of the decree were inscribed on stone, one at Actium (now lost) and this one at Olympia, of local grey limestone, 1·49 m high, with 77 lines of carefully inscribed text. It was found in two pieces, almost complete, in 1954 and 1955. Olympia had no connection with the Actian Games, which were unimportant local Games; the deposition of this decree there is thus an example of a common custom of solemnizing public documents by placing copies in the great pan-Hellenic shrine of Zeus (see p. 100). After Augustus defeated Antony and Cleopatra at Actium in 31 B.C., the Actian Games were elevated to Circuit status (see p. 110 and Plate 2b).

(a) A model by P. Schazmann.

PLATE 28 The largest gymnasium in the Greek world, in Pergamum in Asia Minor. It was originally constructed about 1 B.C. and several times modified and added to. Shown here is the structure in the second century A.D., by which time there w five other gymnasia in the city. It was constructed on the south-eastern slope of the acropolis, and the terrain required co plicated engineering, especially for the foundations which had to bear so heavy a load on three levels. The lowest terrace, wi a triangular shape determined by the two streets running alongside, is 12 m below the middle one; the upper terrace is anoth 14 m above that. At its maximum, the middle terrace measures 150 by 36 m; the main two-storey building above it is 195·7 wide. The most important buildings were in the upper part: the main temple, a theatre, the palaestra, a covered stadiu and perhaps an open-air hippodrome. Other temples, altars, statuary, colonnades and bathing facilities were scattered throug out. Ramps and stairs provided access from one level to the other, and there was an elaborate water-supply system for fountai and baths.

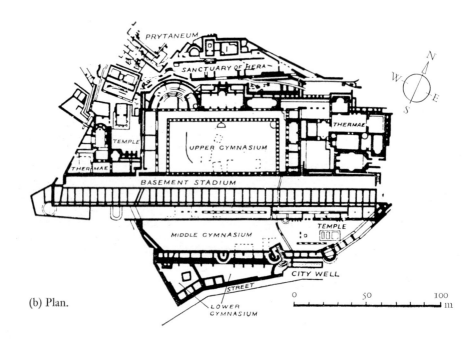

(b) Plan.

PLATE 29   GYMNASIUM (OR PALAESTRA) SCENES

(a) A boy being helped onto a horse, presumably in one of his first riding lessons. As usual there is no saddle and in this case no bridle or reins. The scene is on an Athenian red-figured 'column krater' of the mid-fifth century B.C.

(b) The Greeks were capable of wry humour in their vase paintings. Here a fat youth is being mocked by his slim companion. Another youth is tightening the finger-thong on his javelin, and a fourth is swinging a discus. This Athenian red-figured two-handled cup with stem and base was made about 500 B.C. and is exceptional because it is signed by both the potter, Hischylus, and the painter, Phidippus.

PLATE 30 (a) and (b) Nero, emperor from A.D. 54 until his suicide in 68. He visited Greece in 67 and, at his command, the Olympic Games and the other three 'Circuit' Games were all held in the same year so that he could be *periodonikes*—a winner in all four contests. At Olympia, a musical contest was introduced for the only time, so that Nero could compete, and, not surprisingly, win (see p. 108). In (a) his head crowned with a laurel wreath is shown on a sestertius, minted in Rome in about 65. In (b) he is shown as Apollo, with a laurel wreath on his head, dressed in the traditional robe of a lyre-player and playing the instrument, on a bronze coin minted in Rome in about 65 (about twice actual size).

(c) Hadrian, Roman emperor from A.D. 117 to 138, was the most sympathetic of all emperors to Greek culture. He patronized Games, though he showed indifference to the Olympic Games, and organized, unsuccessfully, rival 'Panhellenic' Games in Athens (see pp. 111-12). A rare bronze coin from Elis, late in Hadrian's reign (shown about twice actual size), with the head of Zeus on the reverse (see Plate 6a).

(d) Herodes Atticus (*c.* 101-177), an Athenian and a Roman senator and consul, friend of the emperor Marcus Aurelius, scholar, patron of learning and the arts, and probably the wealthiest Greek of his time. Among his benefactions were the first, and very elaborate, water-supply system at Olympia (Fig. 12) and the grandiosely reconstructed Stadium at Delphi (Plate 19a). He was honoured by many statues in Greece, seventeen of them in Attica alone. Of the few which survive, this marble bust, 60 cm high, now in the Louvre, is the finest. It was found near Marathon, where Herodes had the most extensive of his scattered landed estates.

PLATE 31 (a) Gymnasium scene showing one athlete massaging his companion. From an Athenian red-figured cup of the early fifth century B.C.

(b) The gymnasium was known for its proneness to foster pederasty. Here is an overtly pederastic approach by an older man (symbolized by his beard) to a youth. Each wears a white fillet, the former over his right arm, the latter round his shoulders, and a spear stands between them. The scene is on an Athenian black-figured amphora (with the hair painted in purple) of about 540 B.C.

PLATE 32 The bruised head of a boxer. This magnificent portrayal of a
seated figure shows the damage caused by the hard thongs, with scars of cuts on
his nose, cheek and forehead and a cauliflower ear. From a large bronze statue
of the first century B.C., possibly by the Athenian sculptor Apollonius, now in
the Museum of the Diocletian Baths in Rome.

revealing: the trainer is the *tekton* (literally 'carpenter', 'builder') of the athlete; the training itself is, above all, 'toil'.

One especially successful trainer, another Athenian named Melesias, himself a Nemean pankration winner, appears three times in Pindar's surviving odes. In the ode of 460 B.C. celebrating the Olympic victory in the boys' wrestling of Alcimedon, the sixth Circuit winner in his noble family on the island of Aegina, Pindar wrote about Melesias (with a note of apology because Athens and Aegina were in a state of hostility):

> If for Melesias I have run back in my song
> To the fame he wins from young athletes,
> Let no sharp stone of hatred strike me.
> I will tell, too, of this joy he won
> Himself at Nemea,
> And that later he fought with grown men
> In the pankration. (Who knows for himself
> Will more easily teach;
> Not to learn first is folly,
> Since untried men have less weight to their minds.)
> But here is the master, to say beyond others
> The right way for the man to go
> Who would get from the sacred Games
> His heart's desire of glory.
> Now as a gift for him
> Alcimedon wins his thirtieth victory.

After all, potential champions required more constant, personal attention than they could receive from the gymnasium staff. The private trainers thus became as necessary a condition as the public gymnasium for Olympic champions. Pindar's clients had no problem, but poorer boys required subsidies. If Alcibiades' complaints about the riff-raff among Olympic contestants are to be trusted, then presumably some cities, with their pride in victories, had begun to encourage good private trainers and also to offer financial assistance by the middle of the fifth century B.C. However, the first solid documentary evidence we possess—and it may be mere accident that it is the first—is considerably later: about 300 B.C. the municipal assembly of Ephesus voted a grant to a trainer named Therippides, for the training and travel expenses of a youngster who had already won one of the boys' events at the Nemean Games.

We do not know which of the Games Therippides' protégé was aiming at next. It could have been the Olympics, where competitors were regularly accompanied by their trainers, who supervised their final preparations (and they, too, could be flogged and fined if they objected to any of the judges' impromptu exercises), and shouted advice and encouragement from the sidelines while the contest was on. Their contribution to victory, it should be added, was openly acknowledged, rewarded and honoured by their charges, memorialized in the tradition by a crop of tales of mixed credibility. One goes back to the Olympic Games of 520 B.C.: Glaucus was about to give up in the boxing finals, but his trainer successfully spurred him on by shouting, 'One for the plough', reminding him of the day, when still a boy on his father's farm in Euboea, he straightened a bent ploughshare with one punch of his right fist. Then there was Arrachion's trainer, who, when his strangulated charge seemed ready to yield, cried out, 'What a beautiful funeral not to give up at Olympia', a play on the Greek adage, 'What a beautiful funeral to die for the fatherland'.

We unfortunately have hardly any information about trainers' fees. A contemporary of Therippides, Hippomachus of Athens, charged 100 drachmas for a full course. One city in Asia Minor paid the chief trainer in its gymnasium 500 drachmas a year in the same period, another 30 drachmas a month a century later. These are modest sums, when compared, for example, with the prizes offered in the Games, though they were out of reach of a majority of the population. They confirm in one respect, but not in all, the remarks made by the medical writer Galen, in the second century A.D., that most of the trainers of his day were rough, uneducated men. Galen was not an impartial witness, as we shall see, but he was probably right about their social background. Members of the urban élite simply did not take paid employment as a rule, and it must have been the retired athletes from the lower classes who found second careers for themselves as trainers. Herminus' membership certificate offers a bit of unimpeachable evidence: a trainer signed the document on behalf of one of the presidents, who was absent from Naples at the moment, and, as the modern editor comments, 'it is to be hoped that he was more skilled in his trade than in the art of writing'.

For the first 150 to 200 years of the Olympic Games, when neither the gymnasium nor the professional trainer was yet in existence, athletes relied on accumulated experience, their own and that of others. That this is not to be underestimated is shown by Nestor's detailed instructions in the technique of chariot-racing, which we quoted in Chapter 3. The 'natural athlete', a favourite phrase of modern sports writers, is not just someone who is genetically endowed with greater speed, strength or endurance than his fellows; he is also someone who observes, experiments and learns, and then can, if he wishes, pass his knowledge to the next generation. The Spartan winner of the 200-metre sprint in the Olympic Games of 668 B.C., Charmis, is said to have had a special diet of dried figs. Another tradition relates that the Arcadian long-distance champion Dromeus, twice Olympic winner, probably in 484 and 480 B.C., was the first to abandon a cheese diet for heavy meat consumption. That is demonstrably false, but an important truth is buried in these tales: from the beginning of competitive Games athletes tried, persistently and more and more systematically, to improve their performance not only by studying the techniques of their particular sports but also by attending to their physical condition, experimenting with their diet among other things, relying on common sense and empiricism and also on faddism and mysticism. Then came the gymnasium and the trainers, who directly or indirectly introduced an element of science and discipline, and, often enough, of over-subtlety and over-schematism.

The word 'science' is to be taken literally, because a close, though sometimes grudging, association arose between professional training and the development of Greek medical science. That was a necessary consequence of the central place occupied by the gymnasium in Greek civic life, and the story begins with the 'school' of Pythagoras in the second half of the sixth century B.C.

In Croton, one of the Greek colonies in the Italian 'instep', Pythagoras, a philosopher, mathematician and religious mystic, founded a semi-secret sect which rapidly obtained political control of Croton and spread its influence widely. In their search for an ideal way of life, this group stressed, and studied, the body as well as the soul; they sought a proper equilibrium, and though their precepts about hygiene and exercise were still pre-scientific, as in their taboo against eating beans, they gave an important intellectual stimulus to a new line of investigation that quickly spilled over into the field of sports. They had a bit of luck, too. One member of the sect, a mountain of a man named Milo, famous for his meat consumption half a century before Dromeus is supposed to have discovered its efficacy in building up champion athletes, commanded the army of Croton which destroyed neighbouring Sybaris for all time in 511 or 510 B.C. His personal exploits in the battle became legendary; so did his Games record, which was never equalled, thirty-one wrestling victories in the Circuit (which we detailed in Chapter 3).

It could not have escaped the budding professional trainers that the unparalleled Milo was a Pythagorean and a practitioner of Pythagorean hygiene. There is, in fact, a tradition that Pythagoras experimented with a special meat diet for an athlete from his native Samos, named Eurymenes, who won an unidentified Olympic body-contact event, perhaps in 532. Be that as it may, less than a century later, Iccus, an athlete from Tarentum, another South Italian Greek community, Olympic pentathlon champion probably in 444 B.C., afterwards a widely known trainer, wrote the first textbook on training. Not a line survives, but later writers give us a clue to two themes, his special diets and his plea for a moderate way of life, including sexual abstinence during intensive training. The Pythagorean influence is unmistakable.

What began with Iccus continued for some seven hundred years, in a long, diversified series of books and manuals. Nearly all this writing has disappeared, and it receives little attention in modern books about the ancient world, far less than it deserves in view of the importance of the gymnasium, athletics and Games. No doubt the trainer who signed one of the depositions on Herminus' membership certificate would have found the necessity of reading a whole book an intolerable burden. However, despite Galen's sneer, most trainers were sufficiently literate, not a few of them able to write manuals themselves. Another trainer who witnessed Herminus' membership certificate styled himself both 'masseur' and 'gymnast', signifying a scientifically schooled expert, and his handwriting was a respectable one.

There were even model lessons (or do-it-yourself booklets); a fragment of one from Galen's time has turned up on an Egyptian papyrus, in the form of staccato instructions from a wrestling teacher to two pupils in turn, who are carrying out his orders in a practice-match. The technical terminology of the text is obscure but the following is a possible translation of one section: 'You, grip him from below with your right arm. You, bring your hand around to where he grips you from below and set your left foot on his side. You, change your place and clasp him. You, turn round. You, catch hold of him by the balls.'

Another, and of course substantially different, branch of the literature was scientific, the numerous publications of the medical writers. In the nature of their work, they touched on many subjects of immediate interest to athletes and their trainers—diet, muscles and muscle physiology, physiotherapy, the effects of cold and heat or of sweat-baths on the body, and so on. Much of what they discovered and taught, both the false and the true, quickly found its way into the practice of the gymnasia, either from their books or from personal contacts, which were frequently close ones. Galen himself began his career as a doctor for gladiators.

Finally, there were the philosophers and moralists. Games and athletics appear frequently in their writings, though usually from a concern that could scarcely have made any sense to the athletes themselves. Was so much specialization a good or a bad thing? What effect did it have on military skill, on character, on good citizenship? We have already noticed Aristotle's negative answer, and in our final chapter we shall discover that even Milo of Croton was transformed in these intellectual circles from a culture-hero to a horrible example. However, there was one effect of the philosophers which was practical —and pernicious. The habit of reducing everything to principle and then of constructing complicated systems penetrated the practical arts, and sometimes produced rigid, mechanical formulas and procedures. In athletics, some over-learned and over-'theoretical' trainers went in for an inflexible four-day cycle—preparatory exercises on the first day, then intensive ones almost to the breaking-point, followed on the third day by relaxation and on the fourth by moderate training. The cautionary tale is told of Gerenus, an Egyptian wrestler, who won the Olympic prize, perhaps in A.D. 209, went on the town three days later, reported to his trainer the following day that he had a bad hangover, was nevertheless commanded to resume the four-day cycle of exercises and dropped dead from the exertion.

That story appears in the fullest ancient work on gymnastics to survive (by the lucky find of a manuscript near Constantinople in 1844). The author, Philostratus, a contemporary of Gerenus whose gravestone, he says, can be seen on the road from Athens to Eleusis, was himself neither an athlete nor a trainer but a 'sophist', a popularizer of philosophy and ethics. In the right hands, he believed, training was a proper 'science'. He gave a whole series of proposals for rational, as against mechanical, rigidly systematic methods. Special massages and training procedures, for example, were recommended for athletes suffering from too much alcohol, from anxiety and sleeplessness or from 'habitual nocturnal emissions'. They must be helped to recover their lost strength, to get rid of excess sweat, and the like. So must men who have just had sexual intercourse, if they insist on training though they ought not: 'where is the manliness of those who exchange shameful pleasure for wreaths and heralds' proclamations?'

Despite his criticism, in sum, Philostratus was a defender of athletics and of trainers, in particular against the doctors. Not surprisingly, the medical profession took a dim view of trainers when they stepped beyond mere games techniques, as of course they did in a large part of their work. Their encroachment, said the doctors, into the fields of hygiene and physiotherapy, in which they were not scientifically trained, was bad for their protégés and bad for society as a whole. This attack reached its climax with Galen, who returned to it in a number of his works. 'Malpractice', a 'fraudulent art', producing mindless, ugly, distorted men—that is typical of his tone and language, and he was able to quote in support the Father of Medicine himself, Hippocrates.

The trainers properly replied that Hippocrates had never given anyone a massage. Yes, answered Galen, although a 'doctor cannot prepare any dishes like a cook, he understands the virtues in each one after it is prepared'. But Galen's was a lonely, ineffectual voice in the world at large. Hardly a single doctor is known to have been on the staff of a gymnasium or of Games before the third century A.D., and then only to deal with broken bones or other injuries, not to work with the athletes who were fit. The monopoly of the trainer was unchallenged.

8

Games, Politics and Patronage

When the heralds fanned out from Olympia to announce the forth-coming Games to all the Greeks, they carried with them the pro-clamation of a sacred truce for a stated period before and after the Games. At first probably restricted to one month either side of the Games, the truce was later extended to two months and then perhaps to three, as athletes and visitors came from greater and greater distances.

The truce never stopped a war, nor indeed were the Eleans so foolishly utopian as to imagine they could achieve that. In their world, wars were endemic, ranging from brief frontier squabbles between two neighbouring cities to such large-scale conflicts as the long war between Athens and Sparta in the last third of the fifth century B.C., the wars between leagues and monarchs in the Hellen-istic period, the wars between Rome and the Hellenistic states, and finally the Roman civil wars for which the Greek east served as a major theatre at times. What the Olympic truce was meant to do, and succeeded in doing, was to prevent wars from disrupting the Games, above all by insuring safe conduct for the thousands, and soon tens of thousands, who wished to travel to Olympia and then back home. Hence only open warfare by or against the Eleans was *forbidden* during the truce and punished by fines according to the 'Olympic law'. Not even the war between Sparta and Elis at the end of the fifth century B.C. prevented the Games from carrying on. Nor, to come down to a somewhat later period, did the frequent wars fought in the Peloponnese between Macedonian kings and Greek cities, when the Eleans are reported to have been in constant fear of armed incursions.

The greatest threat, in fact, came from a conflict which was not even Greek in origin: the spread of the Roman civil wars to the east after the assassination of Julius Caesar led to so much devastation and such consumption of men and resources that even at the Olympic Games the number of events had to be reduced because of financial stringency and shortage of competitors. Herod, king of Judaea, an enthusiast for Greek culture, came to the rescue in 12 B.C. He was appointed President of the Games, a post without precedent, and he supplied so large an endowment that the Games were restored to their normal stature.* Meanwhile, the establishment of the Roman Empire by Augustus brought two centuries of peace which rendered the Olympic truce superfluous in any practical terms. Characteristically, it was a writer in this late age, in the second century A.D., who provides the sole (fictitious) example of the condemnation of a specific war as a violation of the sacred truce, and he chose one that was fought in the fourth century B.C., too far away from Olympia to have affected the Games in the slightest. Earlier politicians and orators, who knew better, restricted their rhetoric about the truce to generalities about Greek unity, kinship and culture.

We speak of a 'sacred truce' because, by definition, everything connected with the Olympic Games was under the patronage of Zeus. Nevertheless, although it would be a mistake to underestimate the deterrent effect of religion on anyone contemplating a violation, it

* Only one other 'president' is recorded in the history of the Olympic Games, a distinguished Rhodian named M. Cocceius Timasarchus, about A.D. 200. The circumstances are unknown, but we can be certain that the extraordinary appointment was accompanied by appropriate financial benevolence.

appears probable that at least as powerful a guarantee of the truce was the universal interest in the Games, coupled with the economic, military and political insignificance of Elis as a state. We remember the case of the Spartan Lichas, who tried to win a victory through a false registration. Sparta was then an enemy of Elis, but, apart from such an extremely rare moment, Games (and not only the Olympic Games) were very important throughout the Greek world, the Elean backwater was not, and so there was no ground for violating the truce. Not even a desire to prevent the participation of a competitor from a rival city was a strong enough incentive; at least there is no case on record.

A sacred pan-Hellenic centre to which official 'sacred embassies' and tens of thousands of private individuals came from all over the Greek world, even if only once in four years, of course provided opportunities for varied activities that had political implications or overtones, though perhaps they should not be labelled 'political' in a strict definition. Treaties and other state documents were not infrequently 'deposited' in Olympia, that is to say, they were inscribed on bronze or stone plaques and publicly displayed 'in perpetuity' (Plate 27). A favourite 'fringe' entertainment was the public oration, and cities were not reluctant to seize the occasion for policy statements they wished to have widely publicized. The treasure-houses of the early period, then the statues and endowed buildings were all also a form of publicity, for both cities and monarchs. And it need scarcely be added that such gatherings offered good cover for quiet diplomatic negotiations.

There was, in short, hardly a limit to the ways in which the passion for athletics and for victories could be capitalized on for ends that were in a broad sense political. Three types will serve to indicate the possibilities.

First, there are two known cases, and one failure, of what may be considered politically motivated 'transfers' of an athlete. Astylus of Croton won both the 200 metres and the long-distance race in 488 B.C., repeated in 484, again in 480 (this time adding a third victory, in the race in armour), but in 484 and 480 he was registered not as a citizen of Croton but as a Syracusan. He may have been a political refugee, but the hand of the ambitious tyrant of Syracuse, Gelon, is visible behind the move. Croton retaliated by converting the house of Astylus into a prison. A century later, another tyrant of Syracuse, Dionysius I, tried to bribe the father of a winner of the boys' boxing event to have his son proclaimed a Syracusan. The offer was contemptuously rejected, and the father proudly recorded his citizenship of Miletus on the statue set up in Olympia. At almost the same time, the city of Ephesus was successful in 'buying' a Cretan long-distance runner on the occasion of his second Olympic victory.

The second example is the inclusion of a champion Olympic pankratiast, G. Perelius Alexander, in an embassy sent by his native Thyatira in Asia Minor to Rome late in the second century A.D. with a petition regarding local road construction and maintenance (a considerable financial burden on the community). Such employment of successful athletes had a long history: the first instance on record is that of the Olympic pentathlon winner of 488 B.C., a Locrian named Euthycles. Thyatira obviously hoped that the presence of Perelius Alexander would appeal to an emperor known to be favourable to Greek Games, and they would have been helped by the fact that their champion belonged to a local élite family, held the priesthood of Apollo and was presumably well educated.

Finally, there is the instance of the cooperation given by the Association of Touring Athletes in A.D. 47 on the occasion of special Games celebrated by Rome's client-king of Commagene and Pontus, in northeastern Asia Minor, in honour of the reigning emperor, Claudius. The latter sent a short letter of appreciation to the Association, which they henceforth quoted in full in their membership certificates.

All this adds up to very little in inter-city or inter-state politics, admittedly. For a serious link between Games and politics in antiquity, we must turn to internal affairs. In that sphere, much depended on the character of the city and its politics, whether it was a genuinely autonomous community, whether or not it was part of a larger state, as in the Hellenistic monarchies and the Roman Empire. What an Alcibiades could achieve politically, helped by his glamorous success in the Olympic chariot-race of 416 B.C., obviously could not be repeated by an Athenian five hundred years later, when Athens, for all its honoured past, had been reduced to just another Greek city subject to the final authority of a Roman provincial governor.

It is also obvious that we cannot measure the 'help' Alcibiades' Olympic record gave him. Such intangibles can never be measured. Nor can their existence be doubted. On what other ground can one explain the 'heroization' of Theogenes of Thasos? He was held to be the son of Heracles (his real father having been a priest of Heracles); hence, walking home from school one day, when he was nine years old, he pulled up a bronze statue in the market-place and carried it home over his shoulder. His own bronze statue in the same market-place (and others were erected in Olympia and Delphi) possessed magical properties: after his death it once killed a man who flogged it as if he were beating up the late Theogenes himself, the Thasians drowned the statue in the sea in punishment for homicide, the earth ceased to bear fruit, the Delphic oracle explained that this was because 'You leave great Theogenes unremembered', the statue was miraculously fished up from the sea, it proved to have magical healing powers, and a cult of Theogenes was established then and there. It was still flourishing in the second century A.D., having spread from Thasos to Thrace and to other Greek communities. A few other athletes also became 'heroes', including the boxer Euthymus to whom Theogenes was condemned to pay a fine for defaulting, and the pankration winner of 408 B.C., Polydamus of Thessaly, taller and stronger even than Milo, whose statue could cure ailments too.

Cult aside, it is impossible to imagine that Theogenes' stupendous athletic achievements made no contribution to his political success after his retirement from Games. Sceptics would have to argue that Greek athletes were the only people in history who never turned to personal advantage the many honours cities heaped on them; the statues erected out of public funds at home, in Olympia, Delphi and elsewhere; the honorary decrees inscribed on stone or metal and displayed, sometimes for many years, in one public place or another; the honorary citizenship offered to outstanding athletes from other cities; not to mention the material awards, such as pensions, subsidies and even, on some occasions, payment of the fines incurred for breach of the rules in sacred Games. We may cheerfully leave such scepticism aside. Even the hard-headed leadership of the professional association officially praised one of its members, as late as the second century A.D., because 'in each Game he made his renowned mother-city famous by the herald's proclamations and the wreaths'. Pindar would have applauded the sentiment.

Not every outstanding athlete had an interest in politics, of course, and some delayed their entry into that field until age compelled them to retire from the Games—Theogenes, for example, whose Games record over a period of more than twenty years left him with neither the time nor the energy to spare for public affairs. In contrast, a certain Polemaeus, from Colophon in Asia Minor, in about 100 B.C. abandoned an already successful Games career at an early age, went off to study in Rhodes, then one of the centres of philosophy and rhetoric, and returned to Colophon to become one of its leading political figures. At a still later date, there was M. Aurelius Demostratus Damas of Sardis, whom we met earlier, a president and high priest of the professional association when Herminus received his membership certificate, a man of considerable education and of an élite family, who seems to have devoted himself largely, if not entirely, to Games, first as an outstanding competitor and later as an official of the association.

We should have to have much more biographical information to know why any individual chose one or another course. One of Damas' colleagues among the high association officials, M. Aurelius Asclepiades of Alexandria, pankration victor at Olympia and in 33 other sacred Games, honorary member of the Alexandrian Museum (a sort of National Academy of Arts and Sciences), was forced to give up his sport at the age of twenty-five because of injuries (though he returned briefly fourteen or fifteen years later to win once more, in local Games in his native city). Normally we lack this sort of relevant detail. We must therefore fall back on two general statements, both quite secure.

The first is that it was rare for an athlete from a lower-class background, no matter how famous, to achieve political importance in later life. His lack of education, of family and social connections, would have been too grave a handicap in a world in which a man's class was always a major consideration in the political sphere. He might receive honorary citizenship or such a post as 'sacred herald', by no means meaningless honours, often with material perquisites, but politically empty, devoid of authority. The one factor which permitted exceptions was wealth. If such an athlete succeeded in amassing enough money, he had the chance, at least in the centuries after Alexander the Great, of a minor position, membership in the city council, for example, from which he, like his colleagues, was expected to shower benefactions on the community.

In contrast, upper-class athletes—and this is the second generalization—were under severe pressure to throw their prestige into the political balance. The gymnasium played a large part, both when it was closely linked with military training in its earlier phase and later, when it became primarily a sporting, non-military centre. The gymnasium served as a club-house for the 'gilded youth', and, not unlike certain modern clubs, it was a place where the older generation indoctrinated the young in the right views and values, where political contacts were made, political plans were laid and support mobilized. What went on there rarely received mention in the permanent historical record or even in the contemporary speeches in assemblies and councils, but politics have always had that 'invisible' background.

No example can better illustrate the complexity of the interplay between Games and politics than that of Alcibiades. In 415 B.C., the year following his spectacular Olympic triumph, there was a public debate in Athens over a proposal to mount a massive invasion of Sicily, a mere six years after an expensive and difficult ten-year war with Sparta had come to an end. Alcibiades was a leading and very energetic supporter of the proposal, hoping to be selected as one of the generals in the campaign. As is not uncommon, personalities were discussed alongside the issues themselves. Opponents of the expedition concentrated on Alcibiades: he was too young for such a command, they said (although he was in fact about thirty-five), his judgment was warped by his overweening ambition and egoism, he was extravagant in his private affairs and by no means free from trickery. Rumour had it that he had taken horses which a fellow-citizen had hoped to race at Olympia, that he had 'borrowed' sacrificial utensils from the Athenian 'sacred embassy' and used them in a private sacrificial procession he organized on the third day of the Games preceding the official one in honour of Zeus, and more of the same. Alcibiades replied in a speech before the popular assembly, which had the sole power to make the final decision:

> As for those things that are being noised about, they bring honour to my ancestors and myself, benefit to my fatherland. Whereas the Greeks thought our city had been weakened by the war, they now exaggerate our power because of my exceptional performance at the Olympic Games: I entered seven chariots, which no private individual had done before, I won, as well as coming in second and fourth, and I arranged everything in a style appropriate to my victory. . . . A 'folly' can hardly be useless which, paid for privately, brings advantage not only to me but also to the city.

Strained and irrelevant as the argument may seem to us, it was a commonplace at the time. In the following generation, a wealthy Athenian defendant in a complex criminal proceeding involving considerable family property, closed his address to the jury with a peroration:

> Finally, it is right that you should reflect on my father's character. Whenever he wished to spend more than was necessary, it will be

found always to have been on something that would bring honour
to the city. For instance, when he served in the cavalry he pro-
cured not only splendid mounts but also race-horses with which
he won in both the Isthmian and Nemean Games, where the
herald proclaimed the name of our city while he was crowned.

The 415 debate ended in a massive victory for the 'hawks'. A great
expedition set off for Sicily, with Alcibiades one of the three com-
manding generals. But soon there was a sharp reversal in his fortunes
and he was exiled. His opponents had succeeded in turning public
opinion against him on the ground, among others, that he was 'aiming
at a tyranny'. A *tyrannos*, all too familiar a figure in the Greek world
since the seventh century B.C., was someone who had seized power
through a military coup or trickery or both. The more intelligent
tyrants naturally tried to buttress their unconstitutional position, with
its base in a bodyguard and a mercenary army, by various means
which would gain popular favour, such as public building programmes, conquests—and victory in the main Games. With rare
exceptions, they concentrated on the equestrian events, both because
these were the most noble and the most conspicuous in their deploy-
ment of great wealth and because in these alone they were not
expected to compete in person. An equestrian defeat could always be
blamed on the charioteer or jockey.

The best record was amassed by Hiero of Syracuse, who won the
Olympic horse race in 476 and 472, the chariot race in 468. On the
last occasion Pindar sent him a poetic epistle from Thebes beginning:

> Mighty city of Syracuse!
> Where Ares dwells in depths of war,
> Where men and horses mailed for battle
> Have holy nurture, to you I come
> Bringing from shining Thebes this song. I tell
> How, where the teams of four horses made earth tremble,
> Hiero and his good chariot conquered

PLATE V (a) The pentathlon. This amphora, awarded to the pentathlon winner, illustrates three of the five events — from left to right, the discus, the javelin and the long jump with weights. The other two events were the 200-metre sprint and wrestling. This is one of the earlier Panathenaic amphoras (see p. 56), to be dated shortly before 500 B.C., by the same painter as the amphora shown on Plate VIIa. These amphoras were manufactured on commission from the city and were filled with olive oil collected from the owners of private olive groves which included 'sacred olive trees'.

(b) The sprinter is painted on a Rhodian jar of the middle of the sixth century B.C., 34 cm high. The running style depicted, with the arms bent and swinging fully at the sides, is characteristic of the earlier paintings but disappeared in the course of the sixth century B.C. (contrast Plate VIIa).

PLATE VI An athlete about to throw the javelin, clearly showing
the use of the finger-thong (see also Plates 9a, 14 and Fig. 3).
The pillar at the right may have served to mark the place from
which the throw was made. An Athenian red-figured cup from
the late fifth century B.C.

And wreathed Ortygia* with far-shining crowns,
Where the Lady of Rivers, Artemis, dwells.
She failed him not
When with light hand on the embroidered reins
He broke those young mares in.

Even Athenians who did not know their Pindar could have detected a reminiscence of past tyrants in Alcibiades' boasts. As far back as 640 B.C., one of their own aristocrats named Cylon, son-in-law of the tyrant of nearby Megara, won at the Olympic Games in (exceptionally) the long-distance race, and attempted a coup a few years later. He was unsuccessful, but tyranny finally came to Athens in the last third of the sixth century. For whatever reason, neither the tyrant, Pisistratus, nor his sons played the Olympic theme, although Pisistratus himself mysteriously managed to have someone else's chariot victory 'conceded' to him on one occasion.

These tyrants were still living and working with the traditional aristocratic values, which ordinary people also accepted and welcomed. The later, new-style monarchs, who followed Alexander the Great, claimed royal legitimacy and with it a superiority that put a much smaller premium on personal Olympic victory. Alexander's father, Philip II of Macedon, still thought it valuable to disprove the common Greek view of him as a 'barbarian', and so he scored victories in three successive Olympics, first in the horse race, then with the four-horse chariot and finally with the two-horse chariot. But Alexander, not only a splendid horseman (Plate VIII) but also a good sprinter, is supposed to have retorted, when asked to run in the Olympic Games, 'Only if kings will be my opponents'.

Like the Egyptian Pharaohs before him, an Alexander could not risk defeat, except in war, and his withdrawal from competition became the rule for Hellenistic monarchs, apart from the equestrian events, in which defeat was not, strictly speaking, personal. Roman

* Ortygia is the name of the tip of Syracuse, an island connected to the mainland by a causeway, where the first Greek settlers founded their city.

emperors, of course, never competed, with one famous exception. In A.D. 67, on Nero's instructions special Games were organized for him in the Circuit, at Olympia with such peculiar events (the only time in its history) as a ten-horse chariot race and a musical contest (Plate 30a, b). Not surprisingly, Nero won every event in which he entered, including the two Olympic absurdities. A year later he was dead, and his lunatic Games performance was one of the last in a succession of intolerable actions that led to his assassination. Never did an exception prove a rule more completely.

None of this reduced the popular passion for Games or the active participation of men and boys from all classes of society. But the 'politics' of Games changed radically as politics changed in real life. On the municipal level, the great issues of war and peace had been taken out of the community's hands; a latter-day Alcibiades could no longer trade on his Olympic success for a major military command or an important government post. The office of gymnasiarch or a high priesthood was now the peak of the local scale of honours. One can compile a sizeable list of champion athletes who gained these honorary positions, normally, as has already been said, men who were born in the élite strata anyway.

Further possibilities existed on the Roman imperial level, but they were much rarer. A few athletes were awarded Roman citizenship (which could be held jointly with local citizenship and was much prized by Greeks and other provincials); others were appointed by the emperors as supervisors of local Games for life, still others became 'presidents of the imperial baths' in Rome or 'imperial masseurs'. The Sacred Association of Touring Athletes was the go-between in these appointments, which were strictly honorific though sometimes endowed with perquisites. It is not to be imagined, for example, that Tiberius Claudius Nicophon of Miletus, who was given Roman citizenship and appointed imperial masseur early in the first century A.D., was either a masseur or a trainer in fact. He held the highest municipal offices in his native Miletus, as had his father before him, the 'Milesian giant' whose epigram we quoted in Chapter 3. For

reasons unknown to us, the emperor singled out the younger Nicophon for recognition, and he did so with an honorary title appropriate
to the man's claim to fame. The honour had nothing in common with
the careers as practising trainers we encountered among retired lower-
class athletes in the preceding chapter.

From the emperor's standpoint, an interest in Games and athletes
had its own significance. Unlike the ancient tyrants, he had constitutional legitimacy (regardless of the fact that Hellenistic monarchies and the Roman as well had their origin in military seizure of
power), and he ruled as an autocrat over an extent of territory beyond
the dreams of even the greatest and most ambitious of the tyrants.
Nevertheless, he too could not survive on the strength of his armies
alone. From 2 B.C., *pater patriae* ('Father of the Fatherland') became
part of the regular titulary of the Roman emperor. Games offered an
ideal opportunity for paternalistic behaviour. In place of wars, wrote
a famous second-century Greek orator Aelius Aristides, in a panegyric
entitled 'To Rome', 'every charming spectacle and an infinite number
of Games have been established'. A few years earlier, the Latin
satirist Juvenal, whose glasses were never rose-tinted, saw the same
situation in a different light:

> Time was when their [the common people's] plebiscite elected
> Generals, heads of state, commanders of legions: but now
> They've pulled in their horns, there's only two things that
>   concern them:
> Bread and Games (*panem et circenses*).

The emperors and their closest advisers would have had no
difficulty in agreeing with both Juvenal and Aelius Aristides. Not
only did they go on until late in the third century founding new
Games in the Greek east and approving an even larger number that
individual cities established, but they brought Greek games to Italy,
where Greek athletes entertained enthusiastic Roman audiences. The
city of Naples, Greek in origin, honoured Augustus with new Games
as early as A.D. 2. In 86 the emperor Domitian established the quad-

rennial Capitoline Games in Rome itself, which immediately took their place in an enlarged seven-Game Circuit. (The other new-comers, both in Greece itself, were Games in honour of Hera at Argos and the Actian Games, an old local festival raised in status to celebrate the victory in the battle of Actium, 31 B.C., which enabled Augustus to become emperor.) In 138 Antoninus Pius completed the Italian development with Games at Puteoli in the Bay of Naples in honour of the recently deceased Hadrian. Once again, Nero provided the comedy: he founded quinquennial Games in Rome, called them 'Neronian' of course, but did not himself compete until the second occurrence, in 65. They were never held again.

For the athletes, imperial support, in this and other forms, was invaluable, and their loyalty was unswerving through the centuries. There is a pathetic note in the recurrence of the ancient phrases: an honorary inscription for a wrestler who won the boys' contest in unimportant local prize Games late in the second century includes the typical words, 'he wreathed the emperor Commodus'. However, it was serious business when the Association of Touring Athletes sent Claudius a golden wreath to celebrate his conquest of Britain. The emperor thanked them for this 'symbol of your loyalty to me'. That was the way relations were established which led to honorary posts, support for more Games, and permission (at least passive) for steadily increasing prizes and pensions.

There was a conflict of interest inherent in the situation, much as emperors and athletes favoured Games in principle for their own reasons. The emperors, as we saw in an earlier chapter, were disturbed at the mounting costs. The money came from the municipalities, not from the imperial treasury, but the latter could not lightly permit them to go bankrupt through mismanagement, local vanity and pro-digality; imperial patronage and support for local Games were rapidly tied to imperial control. An early third-century A.D. Greek historian, who was also a high official and a Roman senator, summed up the problem in a lengthy speech he attributed to Maecenas, a close friend and chief dispenser of patronage for the first Roman emperor, Augustus. The (fictitious) occasion was a private discussion of policy, in the course of which Maecenas said the following:

> The cities should not waste their resources on expenditure for a large number and variety of Games, lest they exhaust themselves in futile exertions and quarrel over unreasonable desires for glory. They should of course have their festivals and spectacles . . . but not to the extent of ruining both the public treasury and private estates . . . or of awarding 'rations' for life to everyone without exception who is victorious in any Game. . . . The prizes which are offered are sufficient, except for victors in the Olympic or Pythian Games or in Games here in Rome. Only these should receive rations, then the cities will not wear themselves out to no purpose, nor will anyone go into training unless he has a chance of winning.

The compliment to the Olympic Games is significant, all the more so because it was paid in the third century A.D. Another writer of the same period commented that the Olympic management continued to uphold the ancient standards of strict efficiency and honesty. His judgment is confirmed by the fact that not a single instance is on record when an emperor appointed a supervisor or commissioner or financial controller for Olympia. Nor were financial rescue operations needed there—the exceptional intervention by King Herod of Judaea arose from unusual, and unique, circumstances entirely out of the control of Elis. Benefactions were welcomed, and were generously contributed, but that was another matter.

Another kind of compliment was the practice of raising the status of other Games by calling them 'Olympic', sometimes 'equal-Olympic', and modelling their programmes and rules as closely as possible on the genuine Olympics. One rather spectacular failure points up the implications because the sponsor was Hadrian, an emperor of a very different stamp from Nero. Of all Roman emperors, Hadrian was the most devoted to Greek culture (Plate 30c). In 131 or 132 he decided to create a sort of all-Greek union within the Empire, with its centre in

Athens, the Greek city with the greatest cultural tradition and fame. Among other measures to this end, he stimulated the creation of both Panhellenic and new 'Olympic' Games in Athens. Old Olympia would not do for his grandiose vision: the backwardness and relative inaccessibility of Elis, a source of strength for the Games in the early days, were now a handicap, in an era in which bygone political considerations carried no weight.

There is no need to try to guess Hadrian's long-range intentions; the actual consequences are a matter of record. The athletes themselves refused to abandon the original Olympic Games or to co-operate in any downgrading. Many coolly 'sailed past' Athens as a sign of contempt for Hadrian's Panhellenic Games. Some later emperors tried to bring pressure. In about the year 200, one ruled that any victor in sacred Games who refused to compete in the Panhellenic Games should be barred from all other Athenian Games. In vain: Olympia maintained its pre-eminence, without ever offering cash prizes, in the face of all attempts to build up competing Games. Not even the emperors sought to interfere at Olympia itself.

9

The Critics

Melancomas, the boxer we have met earlier, who specialized in winning by endurance, not by knockouts, died suddenly during the practice period for the Games in Naples, perhaps in A.D. 74. The funeral oration was written by another man we have already encountered, the orator Dio 'the Golden-tongued'. Dio took the opportunity to expatiate on the virtues of athletes and an athletic career, greater virtues, he argued, than those of the soldier and the military life. The best athletes would be the best soldiers anyway, because of their superior strength and endurance. Second, athletes always compete with the best from all over the world; soldiers frequently defeat inferior and even untrained opponents. Then, war victors kill their opponents, whereas athletes have to defeat them again and again, as well as anyone else who challenges. And finally, better arms and armour often give victory to the poorer soldiers, whereas athletes have nothing to rely on but their own bodies.

Not very impressive arguments, admittedly, but the main interest in the oration is that they were offered at all. The Roman Empire and the 'Roman peace' had been in existence for a century; the army was a relatively small, purely professional career-group, recruited mainly from the non-Greek regions of the Empire, and the old days, when the Greek citizen proved his valour in defence of his city, had long disappeared. Dio knew that, of course. In fact, he as much as said so in his eulogy: had Melancomas lived in the good old days, his deeds would have matched those of the heroes who captured Troy and who threw back the Persians. Yet the orator took the trouble to make the case, despite its irrelevance, because the arguments adduced about athletics and Games, pro and con, were as unchanging as the Olympic Games themselves.

We do not suggest that Games as such were the subject of major or continuing public debate. Normally people enjoyed the Games, or did not, and left it at that. War, poverty, taxes, politics, not athletics, were the topics of controversy and conflict, then as always. And, inevitably, the discussions and disagreements about athletics that have come down to us were restricted to a narrow circle of intellectuals, the moralists and philosophers. The views of Plato or Aristotle or Cicero had no direct impact on public opinion, nor were they shared by all intellectuals. Those of the Church Fathers are another matter, for then Games became involved in the conflict between Christianity and paganism, which would bring about their final abolition on religious grounds because of their age-old ties with pagan gods and pagan shrines. The Olympic Committee had no answer to the Christians; they had no need to reply to their earlier, Greek or Roman critics. They went on in their old ways, as if the critics did not exist, and the athletes came as before, the spectators came, the 'sacred delegations' from many cities, and the helpful benefactions.

Yet the athletes did not wholly ignore the critics. As we shall see, their claims and their boasts were in effect a direct reply to objectors. Dio's encomium of Melancomas was merely a more literary, more rhetorical formulation of the ideas and values they themselves proclaimed in the public inscriptions they erected, or had put up on their behalf. A contemporary of Melancomas' named Marcus Alfidius, who qualified at an early age for membership in the Association of Victors in World Sacred Games, also died during the Neapolitan Games, cutting short a career of great promise. His colleagues in the

Association who were present in Naples buried him with full honours and then passed a 'decree' designed to 'bear witness to his mother-city' of their 'sorrowful sympathy'. They singled out not only his comely build and his willingness to work hard at his chosen profession (in language that could have come straight from the poems of Pindar), but also his moderation, his gentleness, his 'kindness to everyone', his decorous behaviour. His city, a harbour-town on the west coast of Asia Minor, duly inscribed the decree on a marble plaque two metres high for public display, we do not know where. It was found about ten years ago, let into the porch-floor of a private house.

In the mass, the athletes were not intellectuals but ordinary Greeks, and we must accept that echoes of the moralists' attack reached larger sectors of the population. Diogenes the Cynic once met an athlete who, with his friends and admirers, was celebrating a great victory and boasting that he was the fastest runner in all Greece. Diogenes dismissed him in one sentence: 'But not faster than a rabbit or a deer, and they, the swiftest of the animals, are also the most cowardly.' Such rebukes, couched in simple, easily remembered, epigrammatic form, were heard from his disciples and followers for centuries, in the taverns, on the street corners, in the town square, even in the gymnasia, wherever popular preachers and philosophers like Diogenes addressed whoever cared to listen. They were then widely diffused by word of mouth, among the educated and the uneducated alike.

So were the fables, attributed to Aesop, a Thracian slave on the island of Samos in the sixth century B.C., though they were being continually composed by many people in later centuries (and were already well known as a genre among the Babylonians and Hebrews). One day Aesop met a boastful victor in one of the body-contact sports and asked him whether the opponent he had defeated was the stronger man of the two. ' "Don't say that," replied the athlete. "My strength proved to be much greater." "Well, then, you simpleton," said Aesop, "what honour have you earned if, being the stronger, you prevailed over a weaker man? You might be tolerated if you were telling us that by skill you overcame a man who was superior to you in bodily strength." '

Usually these fables and epigrams were told in generalized terms, but more learned writers did not hesitate to pin them to the famous athletes of the tradition. Thus, one of the legends that had grown up about Milo of Croton was that he once picked up a four-year-old bull which had just been sacrificed at Olympia, carried the carcass round the Stadium on his shoulders, then cut it up and consumed it in a single day. 'What surpassing witlessness', wrote Galen the physician, 'not to realize even this much, that a short while before, when the bull was alive, the animal's mind held up its own body with much less exertion than Milo put forth; furthermore, that the bull could even run as it held itself upright. Yet the bull's mind was not worth anything—just about like Milo's.'

Two interlocking themes patently run through all the criticisms: the glorification of the athlete rests on a false evaluation of what is truly and properly human in man, on an exaggeration of certain bodily excellences at the expense of all the rest, bodily as well as mental or spiritual; and, from a civic point of view, the enthusiasm for the professional victors in competitive Games diverts attention from the real needs of the community, for example, from the need for disciplined soldiers. Monotony sets in quickly. There are just so many ways of saying that rabbits run faster and are cowards, that athletes eat too much, or that skill, the application of intelligence, is something to boast about, not natural endowment in muscles or stature. A feeling of unreality also begins to creep in quickly. Neither the practice of the athletes themselves nor the popularity of the Games shows any sign of being affected, let alone harmed, by the critics. Gentleness may be a virtue in an epitaph; cauliflower ears are a better witness to the realities while a boxer is alive (Plate 32). In another of his satirical epigrams, Lucillius mocked an Olympic boxer. Once he had a nose, a chin, a forehead, ears and eyelids; now he has been deprived of his inheritance, for his brother accused him of being an impostor and, as proof, produced a portrait to which he no longer bore any resemblance.

However, bad jokes should not mislead us. There was serious social criticism underneath the repetitive complaints, criticism that was closely linked with important social and political problems of the day and yet is timeless, recurring whenever and wherever athletic contests are a popular feature of social life. That the criticisms had little visible effect in practice is itself worthy of note. Juvenal was not joking when he rebuked the plebs: once you 'elected generals, heads of state, commanders of legions', now you care only for bread and the Games. But Juvenal was also fatalistic: Roman emperors encouraged 'bread and circuses', they wanted no part of popular elections or any other form of popular participation in government, and he knew it. Juvenal's ancient Greek predecessors, however, in the days of the autonomous free cities, were raising immediately meaningful questions on the same theme, whether anyone listened or not.

The first clear voice was heard as far back as the seventh century B.C., when the Olympic Games were already in existence but before the other Games of the Circuit had even been established. The voice was that of the Spartan 'war poet' Tyrtaeus: 'I would neither call a man to mind for the valour of his feet or his wrestling . . . for a man is not good in war if he does not stand firm in the sight of bloody slaughter and strike at the enemy from close to hand. That is virtue, the fairest and the noblest prize in the world for a young man to bring back.' A century later the attack was broadened from the narrower martial test, in a famous 'elegy' that was still being quoted more than 700 years later (by Galen and others). The author was Xenophanes, one of the first of the radical Greek moralists who challenged the very foundation of traditional values. The poem can be dated to the years immediately before 520 B.C.: it mentions the full Olympic programme but not the race in armour, introduced in that year.

> But if a man, in speed of foot victorious
> Or in the pentathlon, in the close of Zeus

By Pisa's stream at Olympia . . .
Honoured is he in the eyes of his fellow-townsmen
   With a seat of honour at Games and festivals
And maintenance at the public cost
   And a gift of treasure from the city . . .
Yet he is not as deserving as I, for our wisdom
   Is better than the strength of men and horses . . .
For though a city had a noble boxer . . .
Never for that would she be better ordered . . .
   Nor her granaries be filled thereby.

Xenophanes was himself an aristocrat, addressing members of his own class and warning them against their tendency to wrap themselves in their Homeric values. There was nothing wrong with Games and athletics, but they had to find their proper place in the scale of values. Of themselves they provided none of the skills or qualities needed in government (Tyrtaeus had made the same point about the new-style warfare). We today may find it difficult to imagine that such things needed saying, but history often exemplifies the powerful attraction of a belief in a 'natural aristocracy'. What else were Theogenes or Alcibiades claiming when they advanced their political careers on the glory of their Games records? Nor did the poets allow Xenophanes to go unchallenged. Pindar repeatedly played up the divine ancestry of his noble athletes; their inherited qualities, without which all their toil and training would have counted for nothing; their heroism, reminiscent of the heroism of Achilles and Jason, and thus of the greatest military glories. They are wise, too, and the choice of Xenophanes' word, *sophia*, is not likely to be accidental.

Even in noble causes the toil and the cost contend
Against a task wrapped in danger.
But if men prosper, their townsmen think them wise.*

* It may be that the ode from which this quotation is taken, the *Fifth Olympian*, was written not by Pindar but by a Sicilian imitator, to celebrate a Sicilian victory in the mule-cart race. But that is irrelevant: such views, and the language in

Pindar's world, however, was on the wane. The traditional aristocracy had lost the monopoly of power, but their boasts of natural superiority survived into Roman imperial times, hollow though they may have sounded to later critics echoing Xenophanes. The upper classes in the Greek cities continued to pride themselves on birth and noble ancestry, and they never abandoned the ideological link of civic leadership with 'wisdom' and athletic prowess. Not all community leaders had first to win their spurs in Games, to be sure, but athletic success, for those who had achieved it, continued to be helpful if they sought active political careers. Likewise, though not all champions turned to politics or community service on their retirement, the athletes, individually and through their professional associations, went on endlessly repeating the old Pindaric language of wisdom, virtue, prowess.

Only one question remained open: were athletics good training for war? The development of the gymnasium, in particular, kept that question alive as a real issue, not as mere nostalgia for a lost past. And on that question there seems to have been a fundamental divide between the average denizen of the gymnasia and the theoreticians. The former naturally argued, and believed, that good athletes made the best soldiers, whereas the latter on the whole maintained and developed the objections first voiced by Tyrtaeus in the early days of hoplite warfare. Thus, in a discussion of the principles of education, Aristotle wrote:

> The athlete's habit of body neither produces a good condition for the general purposes of civic life, nor does it encourage ordinary health and the procreation of children. . . . Some amount of exertion is essential for the best habit, but it must be neither violent nor specialized, as is the case with the athlete. It should rather be a general exertion, directed to all the activities of a free man.

which they were expressed, were shared in this period by many composers of choral odes for Circuit victors.

An older contemporary, Epaminondas of Thebes, who was no philosopher but perhaps the greatest general of his day (killed in battle in 362 B.C.), insisted that agility was more important than strength, and he therefore restricted training sports to running and wrestling (in a standing position), while concentrating on the practice of arms. Epaminondas' outstanding military disciple, King Philip II of Macedon, dismissed Games as a 'theatrical entertainment' (he was not inconsistent when he himself 'competed' in the equestrian contests). Another and later general, the Achaean Philopoemen, who died in 182 B.C., went much further: athletes, he said, ate too much, required too much sleep and a strict routine, all of them impossible for the soldier on campaign, and he ended by barring every form of athletics from his army camps.

A generation after Philopoemen, the Romans converted Greece into a province and there were no more free Greek armies. A Dio might still praise the superiority of athletes over soldiers, but he had to go back more than five hundred years to the Persian Wars, and even further to Achilles and the other Homeric heroes, to make his case. Only some medical men and philosophers continued to concern themselves with the problem of excess, raised by Aristotle, whether in medical or in broader social contexts. Galen would not even allow professional running to have any virtues. He favoured quiet all-round gymnastics and especially exercise with a small ball, on which he wrote a separate essay. A man stood between two rows of players and tried to intercept the ball as they passed it; hence a game in which there were no winners, no contests and no spectators other than friends and family.

It will have been noticed that certain important aspects of the Games escaped the ire of the critics. Barring an isolated voice, such as Galen's, there was no objection to the competitive spirit inherent in Games. Nor was there any to the violence and brutality of the most popular events. How could there have been, in a world in which wars were a regular feature, with their massed hand-to-hand combat, with their slaughter or enslavement of captives, civilian and soldier alike;

a world in which not only slaves were subject to torture and cruel punishments but even free men under the established penal laws?

Nor—and this is vital—did the money-making professionalism come under attack.

> Truly wealth patterned with prowess
> Brings the moment for this or for that,
> If it rouses deep ambition to range afar,
> A transcendent star, the truest light for a man.

Not everyone in antiquity would have said it in just those terms, with Pindar, and many would have protested his choice of a tyrant, Theron of Acragas, as the right man to celebrate in this, or any other, way. But the ancient world was virtually unanimous, save for such odd men out as Diogenes, in its conviction that wealth was a good thing, poverty an evil. In so far as Games were concerned, therefore, both expensive preparation and monetary rewards were taken for granted. Pindar does not make a point of the rewards, nor did the athletes themselves in their own statements of their achievements. This was not a conspiracy of silence; there was neither anything to hide or to be ashamed of, nor anything to defend. There is not one passage in any ancient author criticizing Olympic victors for profiting from their athletic prowess.

A different undertone, however, is to be detected among a minority of aristocrats and intellectuals who disliked the massive entry of lower-class athletes into the victor lists. It does not appear in Pindar only because he was writing before the new development was really visible. But less than half a century after his death we have not only Alcibiades' withdrawal from further competition because he disliked the social origins of many participants, but also some revealing verses by the great Athenian playwright Euripides, a passage that was still being quoted during the Roman Empire along with the critique by Xenophanes.

> For when there are ten thousand ills in Greece,
> There's none that's worse than the whole race of athletes.

THE CRITICS

For, first of all, they learn not to live well,
Nor could they do so; for could any man
Being a slave to his own jaws and appetite
Acquire wealth beyond his father's riches?
Nor yet can they put up with poverty,
Or e'er accommodate themselves to fortune;
And so being unaccustomed to good habits,
They quickly fall into severe distress.
In youth they walk about in fine attire,
And think themselves a credit to the city;
But when old age in all its bitterness
O'ertakes their steps, they roam about the streets
Like ragged cloaks whose nap is all worn off.*

Predictably we find an echo in Galen, who knew the Euripidean verses: 'Perhaps it is because of collecting larger sums of money than anyone else that athletes put on airs. And yet you can see for yourself that all of them are in debt, not only during that period when they are competing, but also when they have quit training. You could never find a single athlete wealthier than a rich man's steward picked at random.' Galen was himself a man of considerable inherited wealth, not noted for his generosity. The point to this undertone of class prejudice is not the moneymaking of professional athletes but their failure to achieve an honourable way of life with their wealth, which they could not hold on to anyway. So Galen concludes: 'Therefore, if you are thinking of preparing to make money safely and honestly, you must train yourself in a profession which can continue throughout life', medicine best of all.

* The passage goes on to make the military argument—does one go to war discus in hand?—and finally to echo Xenophanes about the superiority of wisdom over athletic prowess. It is taken not from a tragedy but from a 'satyr play', *Autolycus*, about which nothing is otherwise known. Lacking any context, we cannot draw any conclusions about Euripides' own views—he wrote a victory ode for Alcibiades in 416 B.C., now lost, probably the last such ode written by anyone— but the more important point is that such negative criticism was in circulation.

PLATE VII (a) and (b) Two running styles. A remarkably accurate portrayal of the difference in technique between (a) sprinters, bunched as at the finish of a closely contested 200-metre race, and (b) long-distance runners, beginning to spread out during a longer run, perhaps the 12-lap, 4800-metre race. The sprinters were painted shortly before 500 B.C. (by the same man who painted the pentathlon competitors on Plate Va) on a Panathenaic amphora (see the note to Plate Va) found in an Etruscan tomb in Vulci. The other amphora, also Panathenaic, with the long-distance runners, nearly two centuries later (it carries a date of 333/2 B.C.), was found in Benghazi, near ancient Cyrene in modern Libya.

PLATE VIII Alexander the Great charging into battle at Issus, where he defeated Darius III, the Persian emperor, in 333 B.C. His father, Philip II, had scored victories in three successive Olympics, but Alexander, though he was a good runner and a splendid horseman, declined to compete in the Games, saying 'Only if kings will be my opponents'. This portrait is from a large mosaic, made about 100 B.C., in the House of the Fauns at Pompeii, now in the Naples National Museum. The original painting, now lost, was by Philoxenus of Eretria, commissioned by Cassander, one of Alexander's generals, and was taken to Rome as booty after the Roman defeat of Macedon in the battle of Pydna in 168 B.C.

Other echoes can be found among Roman writers who had assimilated Greek culture. In his essay on old age, Cicero joined the anti-Milo chorus: 'What cry can be more contemptible than that of Milo of Croton? When an old man he saw some athletes training on the track, looked at his own arms, wept and said, "And these, indeed, are now dead." Not so, you idiot. It is you who are dead, for your nobility came not from yourself but from your trunk and your arms.' The satirist Lucillius, though writing in Greek, reflected the same educated Roman attitude. But the main reasons for Roman hostility to Greek Games lay elsewhere. After all, the Romans were passionate supporters of their own sports, not only of horse-racing but, above all, of gladiatorial combats, which far outstripped anything the Greeks could offer in brutality and bloodshed. When Romans complained that Greek Games were 'infecting' the Roman people, they were unconsciously repeating the author of the Book of Maccabees, as in the outburst by the historian Tacitus against the new Games established in Rome by Nero: 'Traditional morals, already gradually deteriorating, have been utterly ruined by this imported lasciviousness. It makes everything potentially corrupting and corruptible flow into the capital—foreign influences demoralize our young men into shirkers, gymnasts and perverts.'

The crowds were deaf to the plea and continued to pour in, from all classes of society. Romans who settled in the Greek provinces enrolled their sons in the gymnasia if they could afford it, and some became athletes, though they seem not to have been good enough for the Olympic wreaths. The critics were ineffective in practice—yet, as we have already said, the athletes replied to their arguments with a regularity that can quickly become as monotonous as the objections. Galen was answered through Pindar. The old poet described a boy boxer as 'beautiful in body', a boy wrestler as 'lovely to see' (nor did his actions 'dishonour his beauty'), an adult wrestler as 'beautiful, strong of hand, lithe of limb'. Now the boxer Melancomas, in Dio's words, was 'by nature's gift the most beautiful of men', even when seen among 'those who are perhaps the most beautiful men in the world, the athletes'. In the gymnasia of the Roman period, the statues of their patron Heracles showed him as a lithe-limbed youth, not as the muscle-bound, bull-necked man who could stand in for Atlas and hold up the world (Plate 6c). Lucillius the satirist and Galen the physician protested in vain about cauliflower ears, obesity and mindlessness.

Then there were Pindar's 'toil' and 'wisdom'. A decree issued by the athletes' association to honour a retired pankratiast, Callicrates of Aphrodisias, in the second century A.D., reported that he was 'sought after by all people, all over the world, for his perfect wisdom, acquired through constant toil', and proceeded to explain that 'toil' of his kind, involving self-discipline aimed at a worthy goal, reflects the greatness of his soul. A particularly favoured quality was *karteria*, endurance, with the overtone of patience or perseverance, hence again revealing qualities of the soul as well as of the body. The great Theogenes was praised for it in the fifth century B.C., a pankratiast from Smyrna in the first century A.D., an Egyptian boxer late in the second century (and these are only examples).

With endurance (and also *andreia*, courage) we are halfway to a military metaphor. The pankratiast from Smyrna just mentioned was honoured by Olympia itself because, in the final round, which ended in a draw at midnight with an opponent who had had a bye and was therefore fresher, 'he held the view that it was better to sacrifice one's life than abandon the hope of winning the wreath'. An epitaph, recently discovered in the neighbourhood of Olympia, commemorates an Alexandrian boxer, Agathos Daimon, known as 'The Camel', victor in the Nemean Games and elsewhere:

> Here [in Olympia] he died, boxing in the Stadium,
> Having prayed to Zeus for either the wreath or death,
> Aged 35. Farewell.

The language provides more than an accidental echo of a metrical epigram from Elis about a warrior of the late third century B.C.:

There you stood, Chaeronides, among the front-line fighters,
    praying,
'Oh Zeus, give me death or victory in the battle.'

All this is easily dismissed as meaningless verbiage, but that would
be an error. What a man (or his relations) inscribes on his tombstone
is meaningful, no matter how banal or stereotyped it may sound to
another generation. These athletes dedicated a major part of their
lives to a hard, competitive profession, in which their skill was the
most important element, but for which public opinion also counted
both psychologically and materially. They were understandably vain
and boastful of their successes; the only difference in this respect
between a Milo or Pindar's patrons and the men who were memorialized centuries later in the many inscriptions to which we have made
reference, is that the latter lived in an age when there were many
more Games and therefore more victories to boast about, as well as a
greater variety of claims to make. We saw this in an earlier chapter
when we discussed the 'firsts' and the 'nevers' that were being recorded. If there was any change over the centuries, it was only the
growth from the vanity of a small number of aristocratic champions
to the more loudly proclaimed vanity of a far larger number of
champions, many of whom, though by no means all, had been born
among the lowest social classes in the later Greek world.

Their vanity, it is important to stress, was accepted by society at
large as a legitimate human quality. A fourth-century A.D. biography
of Pythagoras alleges that the philosopher once said to an athlete
whom he was training that it was sufficient virtue to train and to
participate in sacred Games, that to strive for victory was unnecessary
and worse, an incitement to envy. Milo (or any other ancient athlete)
would have been astonished to be told that, and the attribution to
Pythagoras is certainly false, just another of the innumerable statements and ideas that the name of Pythagoras accumulated like
barnacles in the thousand years following his death. In the same
thousand years, other criticisms were expressed by an occasional

moralist or satirist, but it would be difficult today to find many examples. The anonymous author of an 'address to athletes', written at the time of Galen or Philostratus, sums up the dominant view: the champion wins immortal glory, he is 'praised' and 'pointed at with the finger', considered as a fellow-citizen by 'the whole world'. We should say he becomes a 'pin-up', and that would also be literally true: when the association took charge of the funeral rites for young Marcus Alfidius, they committed themselves to having his statue erected and his portrait hung up in various places. The practice had become commonplace.

Obviously one had to be a winner, not a mere participant, to be pointed at with the finger. The greater the number of victories and the more high-ranking the better: that is what all those figures we have given were about. Again there was a change in nuance, not in essence, in the course of the centuries. In the old days Pindar could underscore the mercilessness of the victors, the shame of the losers. But as the number of Games grew to many hundreds and large numbers of athletes were competing week in and week out, only the remarkable exceptions could win all the time. The constant Pindaric note, as in his ode for the boy wrestler from Aegina, 'On the limbs of four boys he put away from him / The hateful return, the dishonouring tone', was abandoned. In its place there arose that combination of solidarity and fierce competitiveness that has characterized professional athletes in every society. The formation of a touring athletes' association near the end of the pre-Christian era registered that development formally, institutionally. The association looked after its members in every way that it could, but when the starter's signal was given, it was each man for himself.

Yet the glory and the material rewards were not enough: they felt the need, no doubt subconsciously, for an ideology, a value-system, and it is that which produced the archaic-sounding aristocratic generalities we have been examining. Even under the Roman emperors, the athletes and their spokesmen attached themselves to the ancient Games heroes, their legends and their self-images. Hence the

emphasis on manliness and endurance, on the 'wisdom' that is produced by self-discipline and toil in the gymnasium, on the military
values of athletics and competitions, on civic patriotism (and then on
loyalty to the Emperor). Anachronistic some of this no doubt had
become, but the attraction of high antiquity and unbroken tradition
was all-powerful. And what alternative did they have available to
them? In that sense, the 'gilded youth' retained their sway, even over
those who were, strictly speaking, complete outsiders in birth, wealth
and upbringing.

The anonymous rhetorician we have just quoted cautioned the
athletes he was addressing on one vital point. They must not be
seduced by money into buying and selling victories. That could lead
to various punishments, public disfavour, and, at the worst, exclusion
from the major sacred Games, where the highest glory was to be won,
at Olympia without a cash prize. If, however, they worked hard and
lived moderately, they could count, after their retirement, on a life of
affluence from 'the fruits of their victories'. Olympic wreaths and
affluence remained part of one and the same complex to the very end
of the thousand-year story.

Epilogue

One of the Seven Sages was a Scythian prince named Anacharsis, who went on a journey to Greece from his native land north of the Black Sea early in the sixth century B.C. Whether he was a historical figure or purely legendary cannot be determined, and the question hardly matters, since he quietly became the legendary prototype of the 'noble savage', the mouthpiece through whom a host of Greek writers and moralists expressed *their* views of their own world. The best of the latter was the second-century A.D. satirist Lucian of Samosata (in northern Syria), author of some eighty essays, romances and dialogues, one entitled *Anacharsis* and sub-titled *On Physical Exercises*.

Anacharsis has come to Athens and Solon takes him to the famous gymnasium known as the Lyceum. While observing the ephebes in training, Anacharsis opens the conversation:

'Why do your young men behave like this, Solon? Some of them grappling and tripping each other, some throttling, struggling, intertwining in the mud like so many pigs wallowing. And yet their first proceeding after they have stripped—I noticed that—is to oil and scrape each other quite amicably [Plate 31a]. But then I don't know what comes over them—they put down their heads and begin to push, and crash their foreheads together like a pair of rival rams.

There, look! that one has lifted the other right off his legs, and dropped him on the ground. Now he has fallen on top and will not let him get his head up, but presses it down into the mud; and to finish him off he twines his legs tight round his belly, thrusts his elbow hard against his throat and throttles the wretched victim, who meanwhile is patting his shoulder. That will be a form of supplication; he is asking not to be quite choked to death. . . .

'And here are others, sanded, too, but on their legs, going at each other with blows and kicks. We shall surely see this poor fellow spit out his teeth in a minute; his mouth is full of blood and sand; he has had a blow on the jaw from the other's fist, you see. Why doesn't the official there separate them and put an end to it? I guess that he is an official from his purple; but no, he encourages them, and commends the one who gave that blow. . . .

'Now I want to know what is the good of it all. To me it looks more like madness than anything else.'

Solon explains the function of the gymnasium and then goes on without any transition to the Games and their popularity, to the honour and glory brought by victory. Anacharsis is even more bewildered:

'Why, Solon, that's where the humiliation comes in. They are treated like this not in something like privacy but with all these spectators to watch the affronts they endure, who, I am to believe, count them happy when they see them dripping with blood or being throttled, for such are the happy concomitants of victory. In my country, if a man strikes a citizen, knocks him down or tears his clothes, our elders punish him severely even though there were only one or two witnesses, not like your vast Olympic or Isthmian gatherings. However, though I can't help pitying the competitors, I'm still more astonished at the spectators. You tell me the chief people from all over Greece attend. How can they leave their serious concerns and waste time on such things? How they can like it passes my comprehension—to look on at people being struck and knocked about, dashed to the ground and pounded by one another.'

EPILOGUE

Solon expresses regret that no Games are available to which he could take Anacharsis to see for himself. He continues in language with which we have become familiar: 'You should be there sitting in the midst of the spectators, looking at the men's courage and physical beauty, their marvellous condition, effective skill and invincible strength, their enterprise, their emulation, their unconquerable spirit and their unwearied pursuit of victory.' And he expatiates at length on the value of toil, of endurance and discipline, of competition, in providing the city with citizens of noble spirit and military readiness, 'good guardians of our country and bulwarks of our freedom'.

Anacharsis is not persuaded, and again we recognize some of the arguments. 'I see, Solon. When an enemy invades, you anoint yourselves with oil, dust yourselves over, and go forth sparring at them. They of course cower before you and run away, afraid of getting a handful of your sand in their open mouths, or of your dancing round to get behind them, twining your legs tight round their bellies and throttling them with your elbows rammed well in under their chinpieces. . . . Why, if I were to draw this little dagger at my girdle and run amuck at your collective youth, I could take the gymnasium without more ado. They'd all run away and not dare face the cold steel; they'd skip round the statues, hide behind pillars, and whimper and quake till I laughed again.'

The discussion ends amicably, but altogether indecisively. And the dialogue can be read in opposite ways. One is to accept the Greek view, expressed by Solon, and to dismiss poor Anacharsis as a well-meaning 'barbarian' (as he called himself) who was by nature incapable of apprehending the higher, more subtle level of judging human behaviour characteristic of the best and wisest of the Greeks. Presumably that is what Lucian himself intended to convey: he was a Games enthusiast and went to the Olympic Games at least four times in his life. That is surely how Coubertin would have read it (and perhaps did), and many others since his day, who find in the past a sanctifying mythology for their own values. They have been content to repeat the rhetoric of 'Solon' without ever meeting the arguments adduced on the other side by 'Anacharsis' or Galen. Like 'Solon', too, they slide from physical exercise to Games, with all their superstructure of fierce competition, honour and glory, without examining the logic, if any, of the step.

Not once in the dialogue does Solon even hint at the material rewards of victory in the Games, though he was himself responsible for introducing a schedule of cash bonuses in Athens to back up the wreaths given by the Games managers. In short, Lucian's Solon offers us what may be called the Pindaric ideology of Greek athletic competition, while maintaining total silence about the practice. Coubertin and his associates and followers, like Curtius and the German Kaiser before them, pursued the same road, and in doing so they got the picture wrong.

One of our leading contemporary authorities on ancient sport has recently written that 'the emergence of a class of highly paid professional performers drove the true amateurs out of competition at the top level. . . . When money comes in at the door, sport flies out of the window.' Neither Solon nor any other Greek (or Roman) ever said anything that justifies that judgment, for the simple reason that it is false on several counts. The 'true amateur' never existed in antiquity. Nor did the class of wealthy 'aristocrats' who provided the original, misnamed 'true amateurs' cease to compete, and win, at the top level right to the end of the ancient Games story. And, finally, what can it mean to say that 'sport flies out of the window'? The crowds who attended the Games would have howled at that sentiment in derision. There was an amount of bribery and corruption, to be sure, but the ancient authorities were agreed that the Olympic Games were about as free from these vices as any human enterprise can be. It was, after all, a 'true amateur', Nestor's son, who won the chariot-race in the funeral games for Patroclus by crowding Menelaus off course, the first case of cheating on record. Nor is sport the only activity, then or now, in which competition and rewards breed a measure of corruption.

What was missing in antiquity, because of the nature of the society and its economy, was commercial exploitation of and by athletes. The money which they competed for was provided by direct subsidies, primarily from cities and rulers, but also by wealthy private patrons, who themselves sought prestige, honour, political advantage from their association with champions, but not profits. Paradoxically, this political side of the Games did not lead to national teams, or even to national (or municipal) selection of the entries. The athletes were patriotic enough, as their accounts of themselves testify, and they depended on the state, or rather on states, for their prizes, and in a majority of cases, for their training. Yet in a sense their activity was wholly one of individual enterprise. Their relations with Zeus, Heracles and the other divinities—and we should recall once again that the most prestigious Games were religious celebrations—had the same mixture of self-reliance and subordination.

What we choose to think about sport in the modern world, in sum, has to be worked out and defended from modern values and modern conditions. Harking back to the ancient Greek Olympics has produced both bad history and bad arguments. It may be right or it may be wrong to forbid Olympic athletes to profit financially from their medals, but the answer will not be found in the northwestern corner of the Peloponnese, and surely not when what happened there two thousand years ago is distorted and perverted to fit one or another modern ideology. International games foster international amity—that has been one of the favourite 'historical' arguments. But no one said that in antiquity; in so far as they thought in those terms at all, they said the opposite. In an earlier chapter we quoted from the lengthy eulogy of the Roman emperors by the Greek orator Aelius Aristides: you have brought world peace, so that instead of wars we now have 'every charming spectacle and an infinite number of Games'.

Index

INDEX

INDEX

INDEX

INDEX